PROJECT AIR FORCE

T0097386

Enhancing Performance Under Stress

Stress Inoculation Training for Battlefield Airmen

Sean Robson, Thomas Manacapilli

Prepared for the United States Air Force

For more information on this publication, visit www.rand.org/t/rr750

Library of Congress Cataloging-in-Publication Data

Robson, Sean.

  Enhancing performance under stress : stress inoculation training in battlefield airmen / Sean Robson, Thomas Manacapilli.

    pages cm

  ISBN 978-0-8330-7844-5 (pbk. : alk. paper)

  1. United States. Air Force—Airmen—Training of. 2. Aeronautics, Military—Study and teaching—United States. 3. United States. Air Force. Air Education and Training Command. I. Manacapilli, Thomas. II. Title.

  UG638.R63 2014

  358.4'15—dc23

                                                                      2014003501

Published by the RAND Corporation, Santa Monica, Calif.

© Copyright 2014 RAND Corporation

RAND® is a registered trademark.

Support RAND
Make a tax-deductible charitable contribution at
www.rand.org/giving/contribute

www.rand.org

Preface

The U.S. Air Force continuously strives to ensure that all of its airmen receive the best training available to meet mission requirements. In some career specialties, such as battlefield airmen, the mission requires performing in stressful and sometimes life-threatening environments. To ensure that these battlefield airmen are optimally trained to perform under stress, RAND was asked to review the empirical literature and the state-of-the-art for stress inoculation training.

The research described in this report extended over 11 months, from September 2010 through August 2011. The project was commissioned by Air Education and Training Command (AETC/A2/3/10). The research was conducted within the Manpower, Personnel, and Training program of RAND Project AIR FORCE.

This report should be of interest to military leaders, trainers, and psychologists concerned with training methods for optimizing military personnel performance under stress.

RAND Project Air Force

RAND Project AIR FORCE (PAF), a division of the RAND Corporation, is the U.S. Air Force's federally funded research and development center for studies and analyses. PAF provides the Air Force with independent analyses of policy alternatives affecting the development, employment, combat readiness, and support of current and future air, space, and cyber forces. Research is conducted in four programs: Force Modernization and Employment; Manpower, Personnel, and Training; Resource Management; and Strategy and Doctrine. The research reported here was prepared under contract FA7014-06-C-0001. Further information may be obtained from the Strategic Planning Division, Directorate of Plans, Hq USAF.

Additional information about PAF is available on our website:
http://www.rand.org/paf/

Contents

Figures and Tables

Figures

Tables

Summary

Battlefield airmen serve in several career specialties that require performing under stressful conditions. Two of these specialties in particular, pararescue and combat control, routinely operate outside the wire (i.e., in enemy territory) to recover downed or injured military personnel and direct military aircraft in hostile or denied regions, respectively. Consequently, effective performance in these careers requires the ability to cope with severe stress to ensure that the mission succeeds.

Several strategies can be used to ensure that battlefield airmen are successful and can perform well under stress. First, screening measures can be used to predict and select battlefield airmen who have a higher probability of succeeding in stressful environments. Second, instructors can screen out trainees who are unable to perform successfully under stressful conditions. Third, trainees can self-select out of training if they are unable to cope with the high physical and psychological demands of training. Finally, instructors can educate airmen about stress responses, provide specific behavioral and cognitive skills training, and structure opportunities to practice these skills at different career stages to optimize performance under stress.

Overall, the Air Force uses many successful strategies to ensure that battlefield airmen are successful and perform well under stress. However, some components of the last strategy presented above, termed *stress inoculation training* or *stress exposure training*, and the primary focus of this report, have not been fully incorporated as a deliberate element in training all battlefield airmen. Although battlefield airmen are given sufficient opportunities to develop and practice their technical skills under a variety of conditions, few resources beyond instruction for PJs have been devoted to developing the *cognitive* and *behavioral skills* useful to effectively manage stress. Consequently, not all battlefield airmen may not have developed the full set of skills needed to maintain a high level of performance while under stress. In contrast, the Army and Navy prepare special operators to manage stress by leveraging techniques used to enhance the performance of elite athletes. These skills should be incorporated as part of a three-stage approach to enhance performance under stress:

1. Increase battlefield airmen's conceptual understanding of how stress affects their emotions, thoughts, decisionmaking, and performance.
2. Increase battlefield airmen's repertoire of behavioral and cognitive skills that can aid performance under stress.
3. Provide opportunities for battlefield airmen to practice these new skills while performing job duties under stressful conditions that approximate the operational environment.

Implementation of stress inoculation training could be optimized through coordination with the Army, Navy, and Air Force PJs to develop curricula specific to the needs of all battlefield airmen. Opportunities to deliver training during initial skills training, advanced training, and unit training and before training exercises designed to induce stress should be considered. To further promote readiness, training should continue to incorporate common stressors experienced by those who have deployed.

As a long-term objective, the Air Force should also consider developing a *center* to conduct research and support the optimization of performance under stress. Such a center might include experts from several disciplines (e.g., sports psychology, nutritionists, and physical therapists). These experts could serve as consultants to instructors, commanders, and battlefield airmen to ensure that both mind and body are optimized for performance under stress.

The incorporation of an effective stress inoculation training program would be expected to positively affect mission readiness in several ways, including enhanced performance under stress, reduced attrition during initial skills training, and increased retention of battlefield airmen.

Acknowledgments

We express our thanks to the psychologists and subject matter experts who provided information for this report: from the Department of the Air Force, Elizabeth Heron, Ph.D., MPH (342 TRS PSYCLOPS, Lackland Air Force Base [AFB]); Lt Col Mark Staal, Ph.D. (Chief, Psychological Applications, 24th Special Tactics Squadron); Lt Col James Young, Ph.D. (Chief, Special Operations and Aerospace Psychology, 720th Special Tactics Group); and Lt Col Patrick O'Maille, Ph.D. (Deputy Command Psychologist, Joint Special Operations Command). We also thank, from the Department of the Navy, LT John Price, Psy.D. (Command Psychologist, Naval Special Warfare Center), and CDR Eric Potterat, Ph.D. (U.S. Special Operations Command, Naval Special Warfare Group ONE Headquarters); and from the Department of the Army, Coreen Harada, Ed.D. (Comprehensive Soldier Fitness, Performance and Resilience Enhancement Program); COL Morgan Banks, Ph.D. (Director, Psychological Applications, U.S. Army Special Operations Command); MAJ Bobby Sidell, Psy.D. (Command Psychologists, 1st SWTG, JFK Special Warfare Center and School); and Nancy Wesensten, Ph.D. (Center for Military Psychiatry and Neuroscience, Walter Reed Army Institute of Research).

We also would like to acknowledge the combat controllers, pararescuemen, and trainers who participated in our focus groups and all battlefield airmen and military personnel who risk their lives in service to our country.

We are grateful for the many thoughtful discussions, suggestions, and support from AETC commanders and staff: Col Lee Pittman (AETC AETC/A3T); Col Gregory Reese (AETC 37 TRG/CC); Col James Clark (USAF AETC A3T); Col Bruce Willett (USAF AETC AETC/A3T); Sherry Hernandez (USAF AETC AETC/A3T); Kevin Adelsen (AETC AETC/A3TB); Neal Baumgartner (AETC AETC/A3TH); Richard Handley (AETC AETC/A3TH); and Jessica Calentine (AETC AETC/A3T).

We also extend our gratitude to Bobby Theologis (2LT, USAF, Doctoral Fellow at the Pardee RAND Graduate School), for a thorough review on sleep deprivation.

Last, we wish to thank Dick Hoffman, Rajeev Ramchand, and Robert Sinclair for their thorough reviews and many helpful suggestions.

Abbreviations

AETC	Air Education and Training Command
AFB	Air Force Base
APG	Yuma Proving Ground, Arizona
BUD/S	Basic Underwater Demolition/SEAL Training
CCT	combat control team (combat controller)
EMT	Emergency Medical Technician
FLETC	Federal Law Enforcement Training Center
PAST	Physical Ability Stamina Test
PCS	Permanent Change of Station
PJ	pararescuemen
PTSD	post traumatic stress disorder
SEAL	Sea-Air-Land (combat team)
SET	stress exposure training
SFQC	Special Forces Qualification Course
SIT	stress inoculation training
SOCEP	Special Operations Center for Enhanced Performance
SOWT	special operations weather team
TACP	tactical air control party
TAPAS	Tailored Adaptive Personality Assessment System
VR	virtual reality

CHAPTER ONE

Introduction

Background

Military training has many goals, but the overall objective is clear: to ensure that personnel are prepared to meet mission requirements (Air Force Instruction 36-2201). To accomplish this objective, training aims to develop the necessary competencies in Air Force personnel. These competencies include not only the knowledge to successfully accomplish technical tasks but also the cross-functional skills or competencies necessary to succeed in a complex and often stressful environment. Such competencies may include adaptability, tolerance to stress, perseverance, and attention control (i.e., concentration). However, these competencies have not traditionally been taught or explicitly incorporated into training curricula for military personnel. Despite these gaps in formal curricula, military organizations often try to develop these competencies in other ways. For example, military training organizations may create rigorous training standards that test the mettle and resolve of trainees. These standards often require that trainees execute tasks while exposed to a variety of stressors, both physical and psychological. Despite this emphasis on training under stress, which is an important component of stress inoculation training (SIT), considerably less attention has been placed on developing competencies (i.e., behavioral and cognitive skills) that facilitate successful performance in stressful environments. This skill training represents one component of SIT.[1] In short, SIT is one of several types of stress intervention programs that organizations can use to ensure success under a variety of stressful conditions. SIT is defined by three component stages: (1) education about the stress response, (2) behavioral and skills training to control the stress response (e.g., attention control), and (3) opportunities to practice these skills under representative stressful conditions (e.g., live fire training). As such, SIT is "a set of general principles . . . rather than a set of 'canned' interventions" (Meichenbaum, 2007, p. 8) that provides a flexible approach for dealing with a variety of stressors and intended outcomes. The specific guidelines (i.e., stages) for SIT will be discussed in more detail in Chapter Two.

Battlefield airmen,[2] in particular, serve in several occupational specialties with a relatively high probability of exposure to stress as a result of their routine operations outside the wire (i.e., in enemy territory) (Manacapilli et al., 2007). Acknowledging this increased risk, this report reviews research and best practices for developing those competencies that may help battlefield airmen succeed under a variety of stressful conditions. More specifically, we focus on the

---

[1] SIT and stress exposure training (SET) are used synonymously in this report. However, some differences between SIT and SET exist and are described in Chapter Two.

[2] Enlisted specialties include pararescue (PJ), combat control (combat control team [CCT]), tactical air control (tactical air control party [TACP]), and special operations weather team (SOWT).

training and optimization of performance of two battlefield airmen specialties: pararescue and combat control.

> [P]ararescuemen, also known as PJs, are the only Department of Defense specialty specifically trained and equipped to conduct conventional or unconventional rescue operations. These Battlefield Airmen are the ideal force for personnel recovery and combat search and rescue. A pararescueman's primary function is as a personnel recovery specialist, with emergency medical capabilities in humanitarian and combat environments. They deploy in any available manner, to include air-land-sea tactics, into restricted environments to authenticate, extract, treat, stabilize and evacuate injured personnel, while acting in an enemy-evading, recovery role. PJs participate in search and rescue, combat search and rescue, recovery support for NASA and conduct other operations as appropriate.[3]

Combat controllers, generally referred to as CCTs, are assigned to special tactics squadrons "to deploy undetected into combat and hostile environments to establish assault zones or airfields, while simultaneously conducting air traffic control, fire support, command and control, direct action, counter-terrorism, foreign internal defense, humanitarian assistance and special reconnaissance."[4] We selected PJs and CCTs because these career specialties are known to include stress as an integral component of training (Manacapilli et al., 2007). Additional information on the PJ and CCT training pipeline is provided in a following section on how the Air Force approaches SIT.

The primary question addressed by this research was "Is the Air Force doing everything it can to prepare battlefield airmen to perform successfully under stressful conditions?" Therefore, to the extent that stress is anticipated for other battlefield airmen, the research, general principles, and training approaches presented in this report would certainly apply.

Limitations

This report is not intended to inform issues related to stress and mental health (e.g., post traumatic stress disorder [PTSD], depression, or anxiety). Consequently, we do not review research evaluating the effects of SIT to either treat or prevent psychopathology (e.g., PTSD). In limited cases, we do present findings from research showing that SIT can reduce anxiety; however, it is in the context of maintaining or improving *performance* rather than its effects on mental health or psychological well-being. We refer readers interested in psychological health, resilience, and well-being in the military to other comprehensive reports investigating these issues (e.g., Meredith et al., 2011; Tanielian et al., 2008).

Our intent with the focus groups we conducted with PJs and CCTs was not to generalize the effectiveness of current training methods but simply to identify the existence and nature of any training provided to maintain a high level of performance under stress. Additionally, we did not attempt to generalize our findings on current programs to the broader Air Force. We recognize that numerous efforts are currently being conducted to enhance airmen's resilience

---

[3]   U.S. Air Force, Pararescue fact sheet, February 1, 2012.

[4]   U.S. Air Force, Combat Control fact sheet, August 18, 2010.

or ability to successfully handle adversity. However, the focus of our research was battlefield airmen; other career fields may have different programs to enhance performance under stress.

Organization of This Report

We begin by providing a conceptual overview of SIT. This overview will present the components of SIT followed by specific methods for adapting SIT to a military training context and an evaluation of the effectiveness of SIT for enhancing performance under stress. In subsequent sections, we compare approaches used by the Air Force, Navy, and Army to ensure high levels of performance under stress. Although we provide a broad overview of related strategies used to ensure high levels of performance (e.g., selection of operators), we focus on the cognitive and behavioral skills formally taught during training. We conclude with nine recommendations emphasizing a comprehensive strategy for optimizing mission performance under stress.

CHAPTER TWO

What Is Stress Inoculation?

Overview

Stress has been linked to impaired performance in both civilian and military settings (Driskell, Salas, and Johnston, 1999; Johnston and Cannon-Bowers, 1996; Orasanu and Backer, 1996). The adverse effects of stress on performance have been attributed to altered cognitive processes (e.g., attention, memory, and decisionmaking) (Young, 2008). For example, military personnel experiencing high task loads and time pressures lose a sense of team perspective through narrowed attention, resulting in decreased performance (Driskell, Salas, and Johnston, 1999). Several other types of stressors have also been shown to negatively affect performance, including noise, thermal stress (e.g., heat and cold), and fatigue (Staal, 2004).

A variety of concepts and models have been developed to describe and predict how people respond to stress. In general, modern theories of stress emphasize at least two core components influencing how people respond to stress: (1) an appraisal process and (2) self-regulatory systems (Hancock and Szalma, 2008). The appraisal process, emphasized heavily by Lazarus and Folkman (1984), involves an individual's evaluations of potentially stressful situations to determine if he has the ability and resources necessary to effectively cope with the situation. That is, the individual engages in primary appraisal to determine if a threat is present, followed by a secondary appraisal to determine options for coping with the threat (Adler et al., 2004). Therefore, the situation is not inherently stressful but rather it is the person's interpretation of his inability or lack of options to effectively handle the situation that results in stress.

In addition to these appraisals, modern stress theories also emphasize the mechanisms individuals use to control their emotions, thoughts, and behaviors as they encounter potentially threatening situations. These self-regulatory systems are important, in part, for controlling efforts directed toward goal attainment in difficult conditions (Hockey, 1997). Taken together, these processes help explain why some individuals continue to perform well under stress, whereas others make critical errors or even fail to perform. To combat the negative consequences of stress, organizations can provide three general types of interventions: primary, secondary, and tertiary (Lamontagne et al., 2007). Primary interventions aim to reduce exposure to stress by modifying the work environment or removing the stressor. Although this type of stress intervention may be useful in noncombat environments, environments to which participants are deployed are often unpredictable and difficult to control. Secondary interventions involve training to provide education and skill development to improve participants' knowledge, skills, and ability to deal with stressful situations. Finally, tertiary interventions focus on the provision of care and support to those experiencing symptoms from exposure to stress. Ideally, the Air Force would reduce the number of those needing support from tertiary interventions by providing effective primary and secondary interventions. In situations where primary interventions may be difficult to design for airmen deployed to combat environments, emphasis should be placed on secondary interventions that promote the development of cognitive and behavioral skills to manage such environments.

Of the specific secondary interventions, SIT has been proposed as an effective strategy for mitigating the adverse effects of stress. With roots in clinical psychology, SIT attempts to build resistance to stress through cognitive and behavioral skill training and exposure to stressful stimuli. In many ways, stress inoculation is analogous to "medical inoculation against biological diseases" (Meichenbaum, 1985, p. 21), in that individuals are exposed to just enough stress to arouse defenses (e.g., coping skills); however, exposure must not be so great that it overwhelms the individual. Through appropriate exposure to stressors and training on ways to deal with stress, individuals will develop the confidence necessary to handle even greater levels of stress in the future.

The following seven objectives provide the foundation for SIT (Meichenbaum, 1985, p. 22).

1. Teach clients the transactional nature of stress and coping.
2. Train clients to self-monitor maladaptive thoughts, images, feelings, and behaviors in order to facilitate adaptive appraisals.
3. Train clients in problem solving, that is, problem definition, consequence, anticipation, decision making, and feedback evaluation.
4. Model and rehearse direct-action, emotion-regulation, and self-control coping skills.
5. Teach clients how to use maladaptive responses as cues to implement their coping repertoires.
6. Offer practice in in vitro imaginal and in behavioral rehearsal and in vivo graded assignments that become increasingly demanding, to nurture clients' confidence in and utilization of their coping repertoires.
7. Help clients acquire sufficient knowledge, self-understanding, and coping skills to facilitate better ways of handling (un)expected stressful situations.

SIT is typically organized into three distinct phases: (1) conceptualization, (2) skills acquisition and rehearsal, and (3) application and follow-through (see Figure 2.1). We added a fourth phase to emphasize the importance of reviewing and evaluating the effectiveness of SIT provided. The conceptualization phase is designed to teach the individual about the relationship between stress, emotions, and performance. During this phase, trainers encourage individuals to disclose stressful events and identify how they responded to these events and help them evaluate how effective their response was to the situation. This process sets the stage for learning the skills to effectively cope with stress provided in the second phase of training. Once individuals have learned these skills, they are gradually exposed to stressors that they may encounter outside the training environment.

Although SIT is appropriate for use in clinical settings with patients experiencing adverse physical or psychological symptoms (e.g., anxiety), specific features may limit its application to a military training environment. As noted by Driskell and Johnston (1998, p. 197), SIT emphasizes "(a) the intensive therapeutic involvement of a skilled facilitator; (b) one-on-one individualized treatment; (c) a primary emphasis on alleviating anxiety, depression, and anger."

Figure 2.1
Phases of Stress Inoculation Training and Evaluation

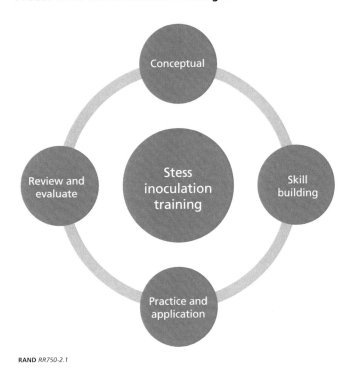

RAND *RR750-2.1*

Using these observations, Driskell and Johnston (1998) outlined the steps necessary to adapt SIT for training in organizational contexts. This slightly modified approach, SET,[1] uses similar objectives to prepare individuals to successfully perform under stress: (1) provide information about the stress environment, (2) develop skills and strategies to effectively overcome or cope with stress, and (3) increase individuals' confidence in their abilities to maintain performance under a variety of stressful conditions.

First Phase of Stress Inoculation Training

The goals of the first phase of SIT are to increase awareness of likely stressors, psychological and physical responses to stress, and the effects of the stress response on performance. For example, trainers might discuss a specific type of equipment failure; how this failure may affect anxiety, heart rate, and breathing; and how these physical and psychological reactions may impair the ability to tie a knot or react to enemy fire.

To fully engage trainees during this first phase, Driskell and Johnston (1998) recommend starting the indoctrination by emphasizing the importance of stress training, possibly through military or civilian case studies of performance failures or accidents that have resulted from increased levels of stress. Instructors can supplement these lectures with field "experiments," in which trainees have to perform a well-learned task under varying levels of stress. For example,

---

[1]   Although the terms SET and SIT can be used interchangeably, we use the original term SIT throughout the remainder of this report.

trainees may have to complete a set of simple tasks when no stressors are present and then when several stressors are present (e.g., noise, flashing lights, or additional information to process). As discussed in more detail below, the Army provides performance feedback and biofeedback to special operations trainees to help them learn how their bodies and minds react to stress. Similarly, the Navy provides extensive scientific instruction on the stress process to increase individuals' familiarity with potential stress reactions.

After trainees have a full appreciation for the potential adverse effects of stress, instructors can begin discussion of specific stressors likely to be experienced during training or when engaged in a mission. Although not all stressors are known, raising awareness of the stress environment can elicit the cognitive and behavioral skills necessary to overcome these stressors. That is, knowing that a specific stressor is likely to occur (e.g., exposure to excessive heat) can prompt the individual to prepare (e.g., drink water and dress appropriately). Indeed, a basic premise underlying the effectiveness of SIT is that "the availability of information or pre-exposure to the stress reduces the novelty of stressful tasks and increases the likelihood of a positive expectation, a greater sense of predictability and control, and a consequent reduction in both physiological and emotional reactivity" (Stetz et al., 2007b, p. 258).

Second Phase of Stress Inoculation Training

The second phase of SIT is to develop cognitive and behavioral skills that facilitate the maintenance or enhancement of performance under stress. Driskell and Johnston (1998) identify several categories of skill training relevant to stress exposure, such as (a) cognitive control strategies, (b) physiological control strategies, (c) overlearning, (d) mental practice, (e) decisionmaking, and (f) team skills.

The goal of cognitive control strategies is to increase attention and concentration on task-relevant performance, while minimizing distractions (e.g., negative thinking). Although there are several specific training strategies to increase cognitive control, attentional training has been successfully used to reduce anxiety and maintain high performance under stress (McClernon et al., 2011). This core feature is developed, in part, on the premise that "worrisome thoughts consume the limited attentional resources of working memory, which are therefore less available for concurrent task processing" (Eysenck et al., 2007, p. 337). Consequently, task-irrelevant thoughts such as fear of failure increase the chances of inefficient and ineffective performance.

A second category of skills focuses on enhancing control over physiological reactions to stress. These skills may include controlled breathing and other relaxation strategies (e.g., muscle relaxation) to reduce tension, heart rate, and nervousness. To aid in the teaching of these skills, instructors may use equipment to measure and provide feedback to trainees on their physiological functioning (e.g., heart rate, blood pressure, muscle tone, and skin conductance) under different stress conditions.

Overlearning represents a third strategy for maintaining performance under stress. This strategy emphasizes repetition of task performance to a point beyond proficiency to solidify knowledge, skills, and abilities. This strategy helps to increase automaticity or the ability to perform on autopilot, which has been recommended as a potential method to minimize the adverse effects of stress (Kivimaki and Lusa, 1994). Although overlearning may increase knowledge and skill retention (Rohrer et al., 2005) and may help maintain performance under stress (Staal, 2004), concerns have been raised that overlearning may interfere with the ability to adapt to novel situations (Driskell, Willis, and Copper, 1992). Acknowledging the potential limitations of overlearning, Keinen and Friedland (1996) suggest that overlearning should not be used when a response is useful only in a specific situation, resulting in the need to change the response. Similarly, overlearning is also not recommended when several well-learned responses may compete with one another. These limitations notwithstanding, overlearning may be appropriate in situations where individuals must respond in the same way every time (e.g., checking safety equipment).

Mental practice is a specific type of strategy used extensively by elite athletes to prepare for competition by mentally rehearsing specific skills and performance elements. This strategy, also known as imagery rehearsal, has been advocated to manage the stress of rehabilitation from a sports injury (Driediger, Hall, and Callow, 2006) and has been associated with better performance (Driskell, Copper, and Moran, 1994; Hinshaw, 1991). More specifically, mental practice is most beneficial for tasks requiring considerable cognitive effort and has its strongest effects when delays between mental practice and performance are minimized (Driskell, Copper, and Moran, 1994). Consequently, mental practice may be most appropriate for trainees preparing to execute complex and cognitively loaded tasks.

Decisionmaking and prioritization skills can also complement performance during stressful conditions. Complex operational environments can present significant demands, which threaten the successful completion of mission requirements. Such demands may include information overload, multiple high-priority tasks, and increased time pressures. These stress demands are specifically targeted through training programs to enhance decisionmaking and prioritization skills. Decisionmaking skills may include the more traditional and systematic evaluation of information and alternatives in addition to hypervigilant decisionmaking. This latter type of decisionmaking involves making rapid decisions following a nonsystematic search for information, consideration of a few alternatives, and swift evaluation of available information. Although this process may appear counterintuitive, research has demonstrated its value in enhancing performance under specific situations characterized by time pressure, potentially conflicting information, and consequences for errors in decisionmaking (Johnston, Driskell, and Salas, 1997). Alternative decisionmaking models may also be necessary when there are more than a finite number of mutually exclusive solutions and the anticipated outcomes of alternatives are not clear (Baumann and Deber, 1989).

Finally, team skills are particularly important in occupations where critical tasks are interdependent. That is, team skills are essential when mission performance depends on effective communication, coordination of actions, and timely performance feedback. Indeed, meta-analytic reviews have clearly demonstrated that important outcomes can be improved by team training. Team performance may be especially vulnerable to stress, as individuals are prone to become less sensitive to social cues. Narrowed attention under conditions of stress has been widely documented and has been implicated in the failure of many teams (Driskell, Salas, and Johnston, 1999). To prepare teams to mitigate the effects of stress, research suggests that teams need to develop cognitive structures that facilitate the sharing of critical information (Burke et al., 2008). One such model, based on transactive memory systems, proposes that individual team members should be aware of other team members' knowledge and expertise (Ellis, 2006). This awareness facilitates the identification of individual team members most likely to contribute to success in a given situation.

However, teams may not always respond negatively to stress. In fact, recent research suggests that teams may react differently to different types of stress. For example, Drach-Zahavy and Freund (2007) found that mechanistic teams do well responding to quantitative stressors (e.g., time pressure) whereas organic team structures respond well to qualitative or complex stressors. These findings suggest that airmen should learn to recognize the type of stress they are facing to best structure their team for success. Other team skills relevant to battlefield airmen may also be found in the numerous reviews and research literature on team learning and effectiveness (Ellis et al., 2005; LePine et al., 2008; Mathieu et al., 2008).

Several other skills relevant to enhancing performance under stress have been used in preparing elite athletes for competition. These skills, used by the Navy and Army, are described in more detail in later sections.

Third Phase of Stress Inoculation Training

After successfully acquiring the skills needed to perform effectively under stress, individuals begin to train under conditions that closely simulate the operational environment. Exposure to these stressors allows individuals to practice and reinforce the skills learned during the second phase. In this phase, it is important to identify the full range of stressors that might be experienced during a mission. Many of these stressors may be general, such as information overload, time pressure, and ambiguity; other stressors may be specific to a particular mission, such as weather conditions, equipment failure, and translation of a foreign language with dialects unfamiliar to the operators.

Although trainees should experience the full range of stressors during training, initial exposure to multiple stressors simultaneously may interfere with skill acquisition. To optimize the integration of stressors into training, Keinen and Friedland (1996) recommend increasing the intensity of stressors after each successful demonstration of task proficiency. Limited evidence also suggests that this graduated intensity should continue to a ceiling, which has been previously communicated to trainees. Without this ceiling, trainees "might develop exaggerated expectations about the severity of future stressors" (p. 264).

Research Evidence on SIT and SET

In addition to our review of the specific cognitive and behavioral skills that can enhance performance, presented in the previous section, we also reviewed studies evaluating the effectiveness of SIT as a comprehensive approach to performance under stress. To guide this part of our review, we first identified relevant reviews or meta-analyses using the terms *stress inoculation* or *stress exposure training*, using the database PsycINFO. Next, we attempted to identify additional research studies that specifically examine the effects of SIT on performance. Relative to studies focused on the prevention of stress-related disorders (e.g., PTSD), very few studies focused specifically on enhancing or maintaining performance under stress. This is not surprising, since SIT was developed as a set of guidelines to treat and prevent clinical disorders. Since few studies examined the performance benefits of SIT as a whole, we also conducted a limited review of specific cognitive and behavioral skills taught by the Army and the Navy; these are discussed in Chapter Three. These skills were most often associated with efforts to enhance the performance of athletes and were typical of sports and exercise psychologists' efforts.[2]

The most comprehensive review of SIT quantitatively combined results from 37 studies using control groups to examine SIT effectiveness (Saunders et al., 1996). The general results revealed that SIT has a moderate to strong effect on reducing performance anxiety and state anxiety and a moderate effect on improving performance, with effect sizes ranging from .31 to .56. These effect sizes indicate the magnitude of the difference in outcomes (e.g., anxiety) between treatment groups and a control group receiving no SIT. However, it should be noted that the effect size estimates for performance outcomes (n = 9) were based on considerably fewer relationships than state anxiety outcomes were (n = 40).

Supplementary analyses also indicated that SIT was effective for individuals drawn from either high-anxiety or normal-anxiety populations. The effectiveness of training also partially depended on the number of training sessions, with more sessions generally resulting in greater effectiveness. However, the authors noted that between four and seven sessions were needed to achieve mean-level reductions in performance and state anxiety. It is also important to note that less-experienced trainers could effectively provide training. In fact, individuals who were trained by less-experienced trainers (i.e., without a doctoral degree) had slightly stronger results.

Other studies examining the efficacy of SIT in academic settings have also been conducted. For example, in an experimental study using random assignment, Sheehy and Horan (2004) found that SIT was effective in reducing anxiety and stress and in improving performance beyond expectations. Although the data from these studies clearly suggest that SIT can be an effective approach for mitigating anxiety and increasing performance, these studies mostly focus on test anxiety and academic performance, which may have limited generalizability to the military.

More recent studies, however, have shown that SIT can be effective in the military. For example, military personnel with no prior flying experience were found to perform better in a flight task following training if they received SIT than those who did not (McClernon et al., 2011). Although SIT did not significantly improve subjective ratings of stress compared to the control group, flight performance measured by variability from aircraft telemetry data and from flight instructor ratings was superior for the SIT-trained group. These findings build on positive findings from previous work using participants' performance in a flight simulator (McClernon, 2009). Another study focusing on the ability to hold one's breath during cold-water immersion found that individuals provided with psychological skills training (Phase 2 of SIT) significantly increased their breath-hold time compared to a control group, which was matched based on initial breath-hold times (Barwood et al., 2006). Although the control group had a slight decrease in breath-hold times, from 24 seconds to 21 seconds, the psychological skills group increased their time from 25 seconds to 44 seconds.

Although the majority of research suggests that SIT can be a useful strategy for enhancing performance under stress, some studies have failed to generate the same support. However, these studies often have important methodological differences, which could account for discrepant findings. For example, Cigrang, Todd, and Carbone (2000) found no difference

---

[2] Although different in many ways from professional athletes, battlefield airmen and other Special Forces operators are often referred to by the Services as tactical athletes because of the intensity and physical demands required to succeed in their missions.

in graduation rates from Air Force basic military training between those receiving training modeled on SIT and those in a control group who received no training. The study population examined by Cigrang, Todd, and Carbone (2000) is likely to be different from battlefield airmen in several ways. First, the participants' lack of motivation may have partly contributed to the null findings, as all participants had been referred for a psychological evaluation. In addition, the reason for discharging the majority of individuals was largely a result of factors unrelated to the ability to tolerate training stress (e.g., greater than 50 percent of reasons were medical).

Research identifying the critical components of SIT is also lacking. Of those studies examining SIT, we found only one that used a randomized controlled study to compare the relative effectiveness of each stage of SIT (e.g., education, skills training, and exposure) to all three stages combined. In this study of occupational stress among nurses, the combined approach with all three stages was found to be most effective, with skills training (i.e., Phase 2) to be of primary importance (West, Horan, and Games, 1984).

Another potential drawback of SIT is the contention that the effectiveness of training is limited to only those stressors that are known and incorporated into the training. Although many military stressors have been documented (Adler et al., 2004; Pflanz and Sonnek, 2002), deployment environments are dynamic and may present unique stressors. Fortunately, research using participants from a Navy technical school has shown that SIT is effective even when participants performed under novel stressors not included in the training (Driskell, Johnston, and Salas, 2001). Furthermore, training was also effective in preparing participants to perform novel tasks that had not been practiced under the stress. Consequently, the skills learned during SIT appear to be useful for individuals who may have to perform under conditions of uncertainty.

To summarize, research on the effects of SIT for enhancing performance is in its early stages. Most studies have focused on anxiety as an outcome rather than on performance. Furthermore, several questions remain unanswered by the existing research on SIT. More specifically, there is limited research addressing which components of SIT are necessary to achieve its purported benefits. Second, there is limited research attempting to quantify the amount of exposure to stressors that is needed during training. Finally, research to guide the selection of stressors in training is almost nonexistent. Although some research suggests that trainees can generalize training to novel stressors, exposure to certain stressors may be counterproductive or even harmful. Consequently, careful oversight by trained psychologists and medical personnel should be provided to ensure that training is not harmful to airmen. The Air Force may also consider developing a review board to evaluate the type and severity of stressors to which airmen are exposed to ensure that training matches intended goals and complies with ethical principles for psychological intervention.

Despite the limits of current research examining the positive benefits of SIT on performance, the indirect evidence described above suggests that developing specific cognitive and behavioral skills (e.g., mental practice) to enhance performance may be beneficial. Nonetheless, no studies have directly compared these skills to determine their relative effectiveness in enhancing performance under stress.

Several categories of skills have been examined to improve motivation, confidence, and performance in both work and athletic settings. Our review is not meant to be comprehensive but rather illustrative of the different approaches and skills for optimizing performance in a variety of different conditions. Goal-setting is one of the most studied methods for enhancing motivation and performance. Findings clearly show increased motivation and performance when goals are specific and difficult (Locke, 1996; Locke and Latham, 2002). Imagery or visualization has been examined in numerous empirical studies and meta-analytic reviews. In general, these studies demonstrate that imagery is an effective strategy for improving performance and may be more effective for complex tasks requiring multiple steps than for simple motor tasks (Curran and Terry, 2010; Driskell, Copper, and Moran, 1994; Jones and Stuth, 1997). Recent theoretical developments based on the neuropsychological processes that occur during imagery and actual performance suggest that individuals using imagery to enhance performance should strive for functional equivalence (Smith et al., 2007). That is, the imagery experience should closely approximate or simulate the different components of performance, including the speed of performance, the environment, and the tasks that need to be performed.

The specific skills taught by each military service will be outlined in the next chapter. We will also explore the role of technology (i.e., virtual reality) to stress inoculation training in a later chapter.

Related But Different Concepts

In addition to our primary focus on SIT, we also reviewed research on several constructs related to stress inoculation, including resilience and toughening. Each of these constructs has a slightly different focus for building tolerance to stress.

Resilience

The term *resilience* refers to the ability or strength of an individual to endure or recover from a stressful or traumatic event. Much early work on resilience focused on the ability of children to overcome trauma or stress associated with difficult childhoods. Following this initial interest in the 1970s, research has expanded to identify factors that also promote resilience in adults following a crisis (e.g., terrorist attack) (Bonanno, Westphal, and Mancini, 2011) and in military personnel and their families who are routinely faced with stressors related to military life (Meredith et al., 2011). These most recent attempts to adapt research to military contexts emphasize the importance of prevention rather than the treatment of stress symptoms and disorders. In an extensive review of factors that promote resilience, Meredith et al. (2011) identified four primary categories of important factors: (1) individual-level factors (e.g., positive coping, positive affect, positive thinking, realism, behavioral control, physical fitness, and altruism), (2) family-level factors (e.g., emotional ties, communication, support, closeness, nurturing, and adaptability), (3) unit-level factors (e.g., positive command climate, teamwork, and cohesion), and (4) community-level factors (e.g., belongingness, cohesion, connectedness, and collective efficacy).

In reviewing this research, it is clear that some resilience factors are consistent with and would overlap an SIT approach to enhance performance under stress (e.g., behavioral control); others are more relevant to promoting general psychological health and well-being (e.g., emotional ties with family). Consequently, we focus on those cognitive and behavioral skills that directly support performance enhancement under stress.

Mental Toughness

Another related area of research, primarily from the field of sports psychology, examines the influence of mental toughness on performance. Similar to research on resilience, a wide range of factors have been found to make up mental toughness in athletes, including an "unshakeable self-belief, the ability to rebound after failures (resilience), persistence or refusal to quit, coping effectively with adversity and pressure, and retaining concentration in the face of many potential distractions" (Crust, 2007, p. 288).

Further research in this area suggests that early experiences, passive toughening, and active toughening can promote adaptation (Dienstbier, 1989). More specifically, early experiences with stress can promote the development of coping resources and arousal regulation, which facilitates adaptation (Lyons et al., 2009). Indeed, individuals who have experienced some life adversity appear to function the best following exposure to a stressful event (Seery, Holman, and Silver, 2010). However, since prior exposure to trauma has also been found to be an important risk factor for stress reactions, it remains unclear which conditions are necessary to bolster resilience.

Passive toughening through intermittent exposure to stress (e.g., cold temperatures), especially in research using animals, and active toughening through aerobic exercise have also been shown to enhance adaptability. In general, this toughening paradigm suggests that fit and tough individuals do react to stress, which is necessary to promote active coping, but will experience a much quicker decline in physiological arousal following the removal of the stressor than will less-fit or less-tough individuals (Dienstbier, 1989).

In summary, mental toughness may be viewed as one of several factors that can be developed to enhance performance under stress. Through tough and realistic training, individuals should have opportunities for developing arousal regulation and active coping strategies. However, training that does not provide opportunities for recovery between stressful training elements will not lead to toughening. On the contrary, exposure to chronic stress will result in sustained high levels of physiological arousal, which can interfere with adaptation.

Summary of Literature Review

SIT provides one broad method for preparing airmen to perform well in extremely stressful environments. The research, which is based on only a limited number of studies, suggests that SIT can be an effective approach for mitigating the effects of stress. Related research, particularly from sports psychology, has provided additional support for developing the cognitive and behavioral skills that can help manage anxiety in a high-stress environment.

In the next chapter, we will explore how well the Air Force and other Services integrate stress inoculation principles in training to prepare special operators to perform under stress. To structure our analysis, we will pay particular attention to any cognitive and behavioral skills training provided.

CHAPTER THREE

How Do the Services Approach Stress Inoculation Training?

Air Force

Although the Air Force does not have a formal SIT program, it uses a combination of approaches to increase the probability that battlefield airmen will perform well under stress. These approaches include the use of selection criteria for entry into initial skills training, in addition to rigorous training under stressful conditions to eliminate candidates not mentally or physically strong enough. Although these practices have been implemented, there has been a lack of standardization across career fields.

For example, officers who select to enter the Air Force as a Combat Rescue Officer[1] must first undergo a psychological evaluation, which includes a combination of screening on intelligence and personality as well as an interview and behavioral observation. Combat Rescue Officer candidates are also required to complete a range of physical challenges and teamwork evaluations over the course of five days. The final selection is made by a board of at least three voting members for selection into that career field. A similar process is used to select Special Tactics Officers[2] and enlisted airmen who cross-train into the CCT career field. However, these selection processes are not used to select enlistees into the regular CCT and PJ training pipelines.

Following graduation from initial skills training, battlefield airmen are provided with education and briefings on the stress process (i.e., Phase 1 of SIT) and perform their job duties while exposed to a variety of relevant stressors (i.e., Phase 3 of SIT). However, their education is inconsistently applied. Education programs and briefings have been added since 2010, but not all battlefield airmen have received education about the stress process.

In addition to the lack of standardization, focus groups indicated that the Air Force has not standardized formal training to develop cognitive and behavioral skills that may help ensure optimal performance on the battlefield. Rather, a combination of ad hoc techniques provided by training instructors and performance enhancement training provided by a psychologist assigned to support the training of PJs has been the primary training approach to developing cognitive and behavioral skills, which may support performance under stress. Despite sporadic efforts to provide education and cognitive and behavioral skills training, candidates are exposed to a variety of stressors throughout the training pipeline, upgrade training,

---

[1] Combat Rescue Officers lead efforts for full spectrum Personnel Recovery including conventional and unconventional combat rescue operations.

[2] Special Tactics Officers lead Special Tactics operators in the full spectrum of military operations.

and deployment training. This exposure is an important element of SIT and helps to increase confidence and promote mastery of skills.

Methodology

Our approach to investigating stress inoculation was straightforward. We interviewed Air Force instructors from the Air Education and Training Command (AETC) and formed focus groups with small groups of graduated students, combat controllers, and pararescuemen from the Air Force. The primary goal of the focus groups was to identify what preparation, if any, battlefield airmen had to optimize their performance under stress. We also interviewed subject matter experts at AETC, the 37th Training Group (37TRG), and the 24th Special Tactics Squadron. Finally, we reviewed key official training documents, the Career Field Education and Training Plan, and the Plan of Instructions) for pararescue and combat control training. However, only the Plan of Instruction for the PJs contained any content related to stress inoculation. Currently, this instruction by the staff research psychologist covers four hours during the PJ Preparatory/Development Course and six hours over a ten-week period during the PJ Indoctrination Course to introduce topics related to stress and performance enhancement (e.g., motivation, self-efficacy, and locus of control). Although this training is consistent with SIT guidelines, it is not fully supported by instructors, nor is it fully reinforced during later training phases.

We used a semistructured interview protocol to guide discussions in focus group interviews (see Appendixes A and B). Focus groups of graduated students were recruited by a squadron commander and were small; each group consisted of three airmen with similar jobs (n = 18). One group was a mixture of pararescue and combat control. Before we discuss our findings from the focus groups and interviews, we provide an overview of current efforts used by the Air Force to ensure that battlefield airmen are capable of performing well under stress.

Current Efforts to Minimize Effects of Stress

Several strategies are used by the Air Force to maximize the performance of battlefield airmen and ensure high performance under stress. Although most of these strategies are not components of SIT, we present these strategies to give context for how the Air Force strives to ensure that airmen are capable of performing well under stress. These strategies include screening out individuals unable to tolerate stress during initial selection and in training, exposing candidates to a variety of stressors during training (see Figure 3.1), and providing airmen with education and support, both predeployment and postdeployment. We will review how the Air Force currently uses each of these strategies to enhance battlefield airmen's performance.

The Air Force is currently investigating different personality measures, such as the Emotional Quotient Inventory or EQ-I (Bar-On et al., 2000) and the Tailored Adaptive Personality Assessment System (TAPAS) to screen pararescue and combat control recruits before entry into initial skills training. Although these instruments could possibly serve two functions—identifying those who will perform well under stress or identifying those with a predisposition to respond successfully to SIT—additional data collection is needed to verify these propositions.

Current screening standards for pararescue and combat control include meeting the minimum standards on the Physical Ability Stamina Test (PAST). The PAST requirements for PJs are slightly more rigorous than for CCTs (see Table 3.1).

Figure 3.1
Pararescue Training Pipeline from Career Field Training and Education Plan

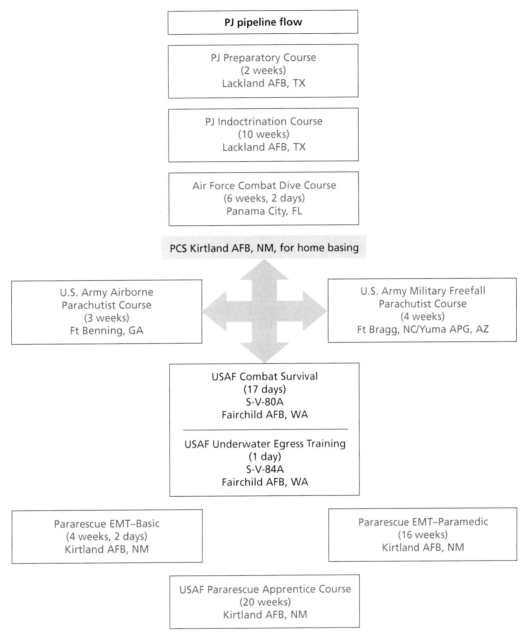

NOTE: Current training pipeline and course sequence at the time of the study.
RAND *RR750-3.1*

Pararescue Preparatory Course. All pararescue candidates must first attend and complete a two-week preparatory course. This course is designed to provide mentoring and coaching to prepare candidates for the physical and mental demands of PJ training. As part of the Preparatory/Development Course, trainees are provided with instruction focused on psychological enhancement. This instruction takes about four hours and includes topics based on sport psychology theory and technique, which may include goal-setting, motivation, self-efficacy, focus on control, teamwork, anxiety, emotional control, persistence, and situational

Table 3.1
PAST Requirements for PJs and CCTs

Event	PJs	CCTs
2 x 25 meter swim underwater	(Pass/fail, 3 min between each) with 10 min rest	(Pass/fail, 3 min between each) with 10 min rest
500 meter swim (freestyle, breaststroke, sidestroke)	Max time 10 min 07 sec with 30 min rest	Max time 11 min 42 sec with 30 min rest
1.5 mile run	Max time 9 min 47 sec with 10 min rest	Max time 10 min 10 sec with 10 min rest
Pullups in 1 min	10 x minimum reps with 3 min rest	8 x minimum reps with 3 min rest
Situps in 2 min	54 x minimum reps with 3 min rest	48 x minimum reps with 3 min rest
Pushups in 2 min	52 x minimum reps with 3 min rest	48 x minimum reps with 3 min rest

NOTE: Current PAST requirements at the time of the study.

awareness. With the oversight of physiologists and swim instructors, trainees learn skills necessary to succeed during the next phase of training, the indoctrination course. CCTs have developed a similar course called the Combat Control Selection Course, which includes screening and initial selection to training.

Technical Training. The training program provides sufficient opportunities to practice job skills under a variety of stressful conditions. However, strategies for stress reduction are provided only to PJs primarily during the initial PJ Indoctrination Course.[3] In most cases, these strategies are learned either on a trial-and-error basis, from other battlefield airmen, or through other nonsystematic ways.

As mentioned above, certain training elements are introduced to enhance confidence and increase the level of stress experienced during training. Two of these particular components, water confidence and sleep deprivation, were identified as important elements to increase task difficulty and the stress of trainees.

Water Confidence. According to the plan of instruction for PJ indoctrination, water confidence training is designed to "build the student's strength and endurance; ability to follow critical instructions with emphasis on attention to details and situational awareness; ability to work through crisis and high levels of stress in the water." It further states that "events are used to ensure they can recognize their reactions to stress in a controlled environment and enable them to better control these reactions when similar stressors are experienced later in their careers." Although several events constitute water confidence training, two characteristic events are drown-proofing and buddy-breathing. In drown-proofing, trainees hands and feet are bound and they must "bob" by sinking to the bottom of the pool, pushing off with their feet, exhaling until they reach the surface, inhale, and repeat. During buddy-breathing, pairs of trainees alternate breathing through a shared snorkel, while being splashed, rolled, and dunked by instructors. This "pool harassment" is designed to simulate rough ocean surf or helicopter rotor wash that may be experienced during an operation.

---

[3] Some recent programs such as BATTLE and Battlefield Airman Camp have been implemented to prepare trainees for the physical and psychological demands of battlefield airmen training. The programs target the preparation of trainees following recruitment in basic military training or as part of the Delayed Entry Program, in which airmen have committed to a job in special operations.

Despite the apparent benefits of water confidence training and other water training activities, email correspondence with AETC subject matter experts identified safety issues concerning the current facility's lack of capacity and insufficient water treatment, which has resulted in documented health concerns, including eye, ear, and upper respiratory diseases. These infections could also increase the risk of training failure and attrition. In addition to these medical concerns, subject matter experts also raised concerns about a lack of pool availability for trainees to practice and develop the water skills necessary to succeed during this portion of training due to reduced opportunities to train in the water.

Sleep Deprivation. Sleep deprivation is part of current Air Force training for pararescue that occurs during the single 22-hour extended training day. Sleep deprivation produces a more stressful environment by requiring that trainees perform tasks while considerably fatigued, however it has a number of negative effects that suggest its usage should be limited. Sleep deprivation is potentially beneficial for helping an individual experience the signs of sleep deprivation, but the effect beyond that is limited by the ability to retain information gained in a sleep-deprived state. Research has not yet been conducted to explore these potential benefits. More specifically, it is not known whether airmen who experience sleep deprivation in a training environment are better able to recognize when their performance is being affected by lack of sleep in a deployed environment.

There are limits to any potential benefits of sleep deprivation training; research indicates that "temporal memory" (memory for when events occur) is significantly disrupted by pretraining sleep loss (Harrison and Horne, 2000; Morris, Williams, and Lubin, 1960; Walker, 2010). Not only is memory affected by sleep deprivation but so is performance, as sleep-deprived individuals show a lower predictive ability of performance (Walker, 2010, p. 50). And, sleep deprivation results in "microsleeps," periods when an individual lapses during times where cognitive performance demand is high (Akerstedt, 1987; Bjerner, 1949; Goel et al., 2009, p. 322; Torsvall and Akerstedt, 1987; Williams, Lubin, and Goodnow, 1959). As Goel et al. (2009) summarize, "(f)ollowing wakefulness in excess of 16 hours, deficits in attention and executive function tasks are demonstrable through well-validated testing protocols" (p. 332).

In fact, sleep is essential for putting learning into long-term memory and preparing the body to learn the next day. Walker (2010) relates that "(w)hen taken together, this collection of findings indicate the critical need for sleep before learning in preparing key neural structures for efficient next-day learning" (p. 51). So, although sleep deprivation training may have some important advantages in helping an individual recognize signs of fatigue, we see no argument for further (increased) use as a stress inoculation tool.

In contrast, ensuring sufficient opportunities for sleep may facilitate the effectiveness of training. Sleep plays a major role in memory processes, allowing the individual to consolidate and strengthen memories, to assimilate and generalize details, and to build informational schemas of knowledge, all of which allow the individual to discover creative next-day solutions to tasks (Walker, 2010, p. 61).

Upgrade Training. Currently, simulations during upgrade training (i.e., advanced training) and as part of on-the-job training are considered as very helpful in preparing individuals for combat stress. The environment mirrors, to the extent possible, actual combat conditions. Multiple sensory events are used to press the combatant. From the discussion, there is no attempt to physically exhaust individuals with unrelated exercises, but rather the scenario itself provides realistic conditions to exhaust the individual. Examples of these exercises include a full mission profile, forward operating base simulation, and the joint readiness training simulation. Each of these exercises provides operators with the opportunity to use their technical skills while being exposed to a variety of stressors typical of the deployed environment. These stressors may include time restrictions, information overload, ambiguous information, and simulated fire.

Education. Predeployment and postdeployment briefings about resilience and the stress response have recently been initiated for operators (and their families) following graduation from technical training. However, this education has not been standardized and is not necessarily provided to all battlefield airmen. When provided, operators may receive education on combat physiology, such as the body's physiological response to stress. Some of these briefings have included an introduction to specific strategies for managing stress, including situational awareness, controlled breathing, attentional conditioning, and muscle control. However, it is unclear the extent to which those operators receiving this briefing have an opportunity to practice or receive feedback on their use of these strategies.

Focus Group and Interview Findings

The focus group discussions were centered on three broad themes: (1) training to manage stress, (2) strategies to manage stress, and (3) perceived ability to perform under stressful conditions. Our findings indicated that very few graduates could remember any initial skills training designed specifically to prepare them for stress. However, all groups mentioned the difficulty, including the physical and mental challenges, of initial skills training (e.g., exposure to stressors). Responses indicated that initial skills training is regarded as a toughening experience, which weeds out those with little motivation. Specific components related to water training, including water confidence and prescuba, were mentioned by three groups as being the most stressful aspects of training. Other specific elements of training found to be stressful included being wet and cold, lack of sleep, and the unknown. Discussions with instructors indicated that these components are designed to put stress on candidates so that they learn to adapt to different conditions and environments. Instructors indicated that they followed a cycle of introducing, reducing, and reintroducing stress into their training. However, one instructor indicated that the introduction of specific stressors is not planned in advance but rather is provided in response to how individuals perform. For example, if a candidate is performing too slowly, instructors may yell and shout at the candidate. It was clear from the focus groups and interviews that candidates in initial skills training receive ample exposure to different stressors but recalled little to no instruction or training on how to manage this stress.

Despite the lack of recollection of formal training to develop cognitive and behavioral skills to manage stress, each group mentioned a variety of strategies that they had learned to cope with stress. Examples included using humor, taking one day at a time, focusing on the moment's outcome, use of logic ("I will pass out before I die"), and positive peer pressure ("I will not be the one to fail on our team"). However, it was unclear how effective these strategies were in maintaining or enhancing airmen performance under stress conditions. In fact, it is quite possible that strategies such as positive peer pressure may push airmen to a point of injury and may possibly reinforce a culture of withholding information about one's current condition, whether physical or psychological.

Participants indicated that they had learned to use these strategies by themselves or informally from other airmen. Since we met only with battlefield airmen who successfully completed training, it was not clear what strategies, if any, were used by airmen who failed training. However, we did talk to a few individuals who failed the program early in their career and then tried again a few years later. The reason given for their eventual success was maturity, rather than any specific training or cognitive or behavioral skill.

Although the focus group participants did not recall formal training to develop cognitive and behavioral skills, the training group psychologist indicated that some time is devoted to introduce stress reduction strategies in weekly instructional periods. As mentioned above, this instruction is part of the six hours devoted to stress inoculation for PJs.

The focus groups represented a very small portion of battlefield airmen, which limits our ability to generalize the effectiveness of current approaches to prepare airmen to maintain high levels of performance under stress. From our limited sample, however, responses indicated that all groups felt very confident and prepared to succeed in operations. This success was attributed, in part, to sufficient opportunities to practice their skills under stressful conditions. This training also led participants to understand that their physical limits were beyond what they had originally thought possible. Consequently, this attribute of training was attributed to high levels of confidence about their ability to perform downrange.

In general, responses also indicated confidence in the quality of airmen who successfully complete training. In some cases, however, we found that airmen were concerned about pressure to decrease standards to meet career field requirements for additional personnel. The implication was that these new graduates may be less well prepared to handle stress. Part of this concern was raised by two groups who mentioned that "quitters" (i.e., individuals who voluntarily decide to quit the training) are allowed to change their minds. In the past, such actions led to an immediate elimination from training, but recent changes provide individuals some time to reconsider and talk to a supervisor first before a self-initiated elimination action is confirmed. Graduates felt that quitters might quit on the battlefield when faced with difficulty or stressful situations. Although none of the participants had any examples to support this perspective, they did not want to take the risk. Despite these concerns, graduates did accept into the fraternity quitters who reentered training at a later date without any concern that they may possibly quit in a battle. A greater level of maturity of those reentering training was provided as the explanation for this apparent contradiction.

Summary

The Air Force, in general, provides some education about stress response; however, this training is provided after graduation from initial skills training. The Air Force also provides sufficient opportunities to perform under stress (i.e., exposure), during indoctrination, in initial skills training and in upgrade training. However, training to develop the cognitive and behavioral skills to enhance performance under stress is limited in scope and structure to PJs and is not standardized to other career specialties. Currently, psychological skills training is not well supported beyond that provided by the psychologist. In contrast, the focus groups indicated that airmen develop their own cognitive and behavioral strategies for managing stress. Despite the apparent success of these self-initiated strategies for managing stress, it is unclear whether they help airmen meet performance goals under stress. To effectively implement an SIT program, specific cognitive and behavioral skills would need to be identified, integrated into training, and reinforced by all levels of battlefield airmen, their commanders, and their instructors. Such a culture change would do well to advance a balanced focus on the mind and the body in preparing battlefield airmen for optimal performance.

Navy SEALs[4]

The Navy has introduced formal curricula for stress inoculation to support the training and development of Navy SEALs. This training is initially provided early in the training cycle and is subsequently reinforced and expanded throughout the training cycle. Despite the recent success in reducing attrition from the training pipeline and commitment to SIT, instructors were not always receptive to the integration of training elements designed by those outside the SEAL community (i.e., psychologists). Consequently, implementation required considerable time and effort to reach its current status.

Methodology

To determine the methods used by the Navy for stress inoculation, we conducted semistructured interviews with psychologists assigned to the training school or with Navy SEAL graduates. The interviews provided the opportunity to discuss optimal points of integration into the training cycle as well as potential barriers to implementation. We also interviewed the former director of education for the Navy SEALs and reviewed concept papers he wrote to better understand early attempts to integrate cognitive skills into training.

General Principles

Similar to many other special operations schools, the Navy recruits individuals who are in excellent physical condition, and many were outstanding athletes in high school. In addition to basic physical fitness requirements, SEAL candidates are also evaluated on a computer adaptive test measuring select personality traits that have been shown to predict who is likely to quit or drop on request. Developed for use by the Navy, this test is designed to screen candidates for special operations schools.

Following boot camp, eligible recruits are sent to the Navy Special Warfare Preparatory School, which offers an eight-week program designed to mentally and physically prepare SEAL candidates for the challenges and intensity of Basic Underwater Demolition/SEAL (BUD/S) training. As part of the preparatory school course, candidates work on both physical (e.g., physical conditioning, swimming, and underwater confidence) and academic components (e.g., exercise science, nutrition, and mental toughness). During this academic component, a Master Chief first introduces SEAL candidates to the four primary cognitive/performance enhancement skills, referred to as the "big four," which constitute approximately 15–20 percent of the dedicated training time. These skills include (1) goal-setting and segmenting, (2) tactical visualization, (3) arousal control, and (4) self-talk. Although specific details of training curricula are classified, we will briefly provide an overview and define each skill.

Goal-setting and segmenting are motivational strategies designed to enhance attention, direction, and mobilization of resources and effort toward an objective. Segmenting, in particular, allows individuals to break apart seemingly unmanageable objectives into smaller, more attainable goals. These skills can be helpful in managing environments that place unrelenting physical and psychological demands on trainees and operators.

Tactical visualization is designed to preempt any stress components by mentally rehearsing performance in anticipated stress situations. This visualization provides candidates with additional confidence when they are able to see themselves succeeding under stress. Further-

---

[4]   Sea-Air-Land (combat team).

more, visualization provides opportunities to mentally practice and prepare for certain performance elements even when live practice opportunities are not available or physical fatigue would otherwise impair performance.

Arousal control, which receives the most comprehensive focus in the Navy's program, aims to control the human response to stress. By controlling breathing, heart rate, and other physiological and psychological responses to stress, it is believed that performance can be controlled in any environment.

Finally, self-talk is a skill used to control one's internal dialogue. The Navy's approach to encouraging positive self-talk is based on the ABC model (Ellis and Dryden, 1987), which represents a method for restructuring irrational thoughts and beliefs. Briefly, the A involves understanding and describing the *activating* event. That is, the individual describes the facts that precipitated feelings of stress or poor performance. Then, the individual documents his internal dialogue and *beliefs* about the situation. Finally, the *consequences* and outcomes of the situation are documented. After fully understanding this process, trainees can then learn how to counter any irrational thoughts and defeatist attitudes with positive self-talk.

These four key skills or pillars are revisited more extensively during BUD/S training, with special emphasis before difficult evolutions in the training cycle such as "Hellweek." Because SEAL candidates are expected to have developed both the necessary physical and mental conditioning to succeed during Hellweek, coaching and encouragement are not provided during this phase. That is, Hellweek is viewed as a testing phase to screen out poor candidates rather than as an opportunity to train and coach individuals on how to use their cognitive skills.

Following successful completion of BUD/S, SEALs are assigned to a team and begin a new cycle of training. This cycle starts with professional development (e.g., sniper, language, and ordnance) followed by unit-level training, which incorporates a variety of realistic training scenarios simulating operational conditions. During these first two training cycles, SEALs are introduced to two additional cognitive skills for managing stress: (1) focused training (e.g., to tune out distractions), and (2) compartmentalization, which provides SEALs with a strategy for managing adverse events by sectioning off affiliated thoughts and emotions about the event, thereby allowing total concentration on the mission.

In summary, the Navy provides training on six key skills to prepare SEALs to maintain optimal performance under a variety of stressful conditions. Although specific data were not provided, interviews with Navy psychologists suggested that training attrition has decreased substantially following the introduction of the prep school and stress inoculation training.

Army Special Forces

The Army has developed an integrated framework for developing Special Forces performance under stress. Key features of this framework include the use of developmental feedback, training support from a center staffed with performance enhancement experts, and the use of structured simulations to evaluate how trainees respond to stress. Interviews with Army psychologists suggested that their integrated approach is successful in ensuring high levels of performance under stress. However, psychologists raised concerns that Special Forces personnel were less well prepared to handle more chronic stressors related to family life and the high operations tempo.

Methodology

To determine the methods used by the Army for stress inoculation, we conducted semistructured interviews with psychologists assigned to support Special Forces training at Ft. Bragg. We also interviewed a senior researcher from the Performance and Enhancement Program, a component of Comprehensive Soldier Fitness and formally part of the Army Center for Enhanced Performance. Finally, we interviewed the Director of the Special Operations Center for Enhanced Performance. This center uses instructors trained in sports psychology to train Special Operations Forces. Taken together, the interviews were used to identify the Army's broad approach to SIT, resources needed, measures for screening and development, and limitations.

Special Forces

The Army uses several strategies, in a Special Forces career cycle, to ensure optimal performance under stress. These strategies include the following: (1) assessment and selection to screen out those with low probability of tolerating stress, (2) training to perform in stressful conditions, (3) use of skills in operational environments, (4) frequent monitoring to identify those having difficulty adapting to stress, and (5) treatment and intervention as needed (e.g., psychological distress).

The first strategy, assessment and selection, is used to ensure that Special Forces candidates meet certain eligibility requirements (e.g., physical fitness) in addition to identifying those who are clearly a poor fit. Consistent with findings from the other Services, the Army has received pressure in the past to increase the number of qualified Special Forces personnel. To meet these staffing requirements, the Army decreased the cutoff on the General Technical subtest of the Armed Services Vocational Battery. According to one Army psychologist, reducing this cutoff has had no effect on the number and quality of those individuals graduating from training. In other words, lowering standards did nothing to meet the demand for additional Special Forces personnel.

After meeting basic eligibility requirements, candidates proceed to the initial selection course. At this time psychologists administer a battery of self-report instruments assessing personality and tolerance to stress. Although the results from these assessments are not used to screen out candidates, follow-up interviews may be conducted by a psychologist to screen out those candidates who are not a good fit. The length of these interviews depends on the specific concerns identified by the psychologist.

Following their initial selection, candidates begin the Special Forces Qualification Course (SFQC). One key feature of the Army's approach is an emphasis on development and performance enhancement. To support these goals, the Army uses its clinical psychologists in addition to candidates' peers to provide developmental feedback to Special Forces candidates and operators. In the SFQC, psychologists join candidates in the field to observe their performance in a series of structured scenarios, which provide the data for feedback later provided to each candidate. In addition to performance observations, psychologists' feedback also draws on results from the self-report instruments completed by candidates during initial selection. The results from these self-report instruments are specifically used to support observations and increase candidates' chances of graduation.

To further support the development of Special Forces candidates, psychologists have collaborated with Special Forces units to construct 360-degree feedback instruments, which provide feedback on performance dimensions related to stress from multiple sources (e.g., peers, subordinates, and commander). The feedback generated from these evaluations is strictly confidential and only the individual being rated has access to the results. The emphasis on confidentiality is helpful in maintaining a developmental rather than a punitive climate.

Although serving a developmental role following selection into the Special Forces community, peers are also used to provide evaluative data on performance during the SFQC. These data are presented with evaluations from instructors and psychologists to advise commanders on final decisions for candidate selections into a Special Forces unit. The psychologists emphasized the value of peer evaluations as an important decision tool, particularly because peers are able to observe attitudes and performance that are otherwise hidden from instructors and commanders.

In summary, the interviews with the psychologists at Ft. Bragg suggested that training needs to be tough and realistic and that waivers must be eliminated to ensure consistency in quality and application of standards. These steps will help ensure that personnel have met a clear set of criteria related to high levels of performance under stress.

Special Operations Center for Enhanced Performance

SOCEP, a center of experts in performance enhancement and sports psychology, was funded in October 2010 to support the training of Special Forces. In general, the goal of the center is to identify the biggest challenges to performance and enhance performance in those areas through training and practice in simulated conditions. Although the curriculum was created by the Army Center for Enhanced Performance at West Point, the stressors integrated into practice sessions are designed using feedback from Special Forces operators who have recently been downrange.

The specific curriculum and length of training depend on an individual's military occupational specialty. In general, the curriculum emphasizes five primary skills to enhance mental strength: (1) building confidence, (2) goal-setting, (3) attention control, (4) energy management, and (5) integrating imagery. In many ways, these core skills are analogous to those used by the Navy to train BUD/S candidates and operators (see Table 3.2). A full description of the Army's definitions of these skills is provided in a Memorandum for Record (Department of the Army, 2011).

Table 3.2
A Comparison of Skills to Optimize Performance Under Stress

Skill	Air Force PJs	Army Special Forces	Navy SEALs	Definition
Mental skills foundation	√	√		Understanding the relationship between performance and psychological states (e.g., thoughts, emotions)
Confidence	√	√		Focus on strategies to build, sustain, and protect confidence; a feeling of self-assurance
Goal-setting	√	√	√	Focus on personally meaningful goals supported by core values; breaking larger objectives into manageable tasks
Attention control/ concentration	√	√	√	Emphasis on understanding how attention works and how to control it to enhance focus and concentration
Energy/ arousal control	√	√	√	Practical skills on managing arousal levels and the stress response to meet the demands of the situation and restoring energy
Imagery/ visualization	√	√	√	Mental rehearsal of successful outcomes to build confidence and promote effectiveness
Self-talk	√		√	Internal dialogue to guide thoughts, emotions, performance, etc.
Compartment-alization	√		√	Dividing or segmenting adverse events or setbacks for later processing

CHAPTER FOUR

Can Virtual Reality Support Stress Inoculation Training?

Technology such as virtual reality (VR) shows promise as a tool to support SIT. This technology offers an alternative platform for the delivery of SIT more broadly. VR, also called virtual simulation, is used often in today's Air Force to train personnel, mostly aircrew. The technology allows aircrew to train in dangerous situations without actually putting the individual or equipment at risk (e.g., an engine stall during a landing) and often at substantially less cost. As the technology has advanced, the virtual images have become more real, introducing the concept *presence* as a way to describe VR (Riva, 2007; Riva, Davide, and IJsselsteijn, 2003; Steuer, 1992). Presence is defined by Steuer (1992) as the "sense of being there" (as cited by Riva, 2008, p. 9) or the sense of being in a different world that exists outside the person (Riva, 2006, 2007, 2008; Riva, Waterworth, and Waterworth, 2004).

The advancement of VR has found many applications in the area of psychology and helping individuals cope with phobias (Wiederhold and Wiederhold, 2008). Medical professionals use VR in exposure therapy, as a way to introduce patients to a safer, less personally threatening, and less costly environment than real life events (Riva, 2005, 2008). The environment is real enough to expose the patient to the feared stimuli in a controlled setting. By doing so, patient's anxiety can be reduced through the processes of habituation and extinction (Riva, 2008). Avoiding the situation only reinforces the phobia.

In a similar manner, VR could be used before deployment for SIT. Similar to the treatment of specific phobias, "VR can enhance the effect of SIT by providing vivid and customizable stimuli" (Wiederhold and Wiederhold, 2008, p. 30). The goal is to provide repeated and controlled exposure to stressors, to desensitize or inoculate the individual to the stimuli, thereby avoiding panic in a real environment (Wiederhold and Wiederhold, 2008). The Army has taken steps to develop VR tools to teach resource management, adaptive thinking, and tactical decisionmaking (Rizzo et al., 2006). For example, the Army has developed Full Spectrum Warrior, a game that is being used for clinical VR treatment of PTSD in returning Iraq War military personnel. This suggests that some existing commercial tools could have value for SIT.

Although the game may have some benefit for SIT, it does not appear to be a worthwhile training aid because "soldiers were disappointed by the game's lack of realism and did not learn the intended lessons" (Adair, 2005). Still, an investment in the game might yield better training outcomes down the road: "The Army officials who ordered Full Spectrum Warrior say it was a useful experiment in how video games can teach urban warfare; feedback about the game will be used to improve other training aids. They expect to save money by using the game's basic architecture to create other games" (Adair, 2005). Therefore, future efforts to enhance the realism of these types of games may improve their overall usefulness for training.

Currently, in precombat use, the tool is used to screen individuals who might be susceptible to PTSD before combat. This use gives medical personnel the opportunity to look for indications of physiological reaction during the VR exposure to determine if the individual requires continued or prescribed care (Rizzo et al., 2006).

But the same tool has potential for SIT.

> . . . such a VR tool initially developed for exposure therapy purposes, offers the potential to be "recycled" for use both in the areas of combat readiness assessment and for stress inoculation. Both of these approaches could provide measures of who might be better prepared for the emotional stress of combat. For example, novice soldiers could be pre-exposed to challenging VR combat stress scenarios delivered via hybrid VR/Real World stress inoculation training protocols as has been reported by Wiederhold & Wiederhold (2005) with combat medics. (Rizzo et al., 2006, p. 9)

The Army's Virtual Reality Medical Center provided VR SIT systems to Ft. Rucker for the Army's Aeromedical Personnel training. VR, in this capacity, is being used to teach coping techniques before deployment, with promising early results (Wiederhold and Wiederhold, 2008). Preliminary results from 25 medics suggest that those who learned coping techniques exhibited lower levels of stress than those in the control group (Stetz et al., 2007a; Wiederhold and Wiederhold, 2008).

Other large-scale studies suggest that VR-enhanced SIT can be more effective than real world training systems, when factors such as cost, time expenditure, adaption to stressful situations, and performance are considered (Wiederhold and Wiederhold, 2008).

Despite the potential benefits, Popovic et al. (2009) surmise that the promising early results of using VR for SIT warrant further research, as the number of available studies is limited.

VR for SIT represents an untapped potential for the Air Force to train battlefield airmen for combat. This tool could be applied across the force, not just for initial skills training. It can provide context for training, making other training more effective and interesting to the recruit. Despite these potential benefits, the application of VR to provide SIT is still nascent and focuses primarily on the final phase of SIT (i.e., Phase 3). Consequently, several questions remain unexplored, including how VR can incorporate the first two phases of SIT, the relative benefits of VR SIT compared to traditional SIT, the cost-effectiveness of VR SIT, and the benefits of VR SIT for enhancing performance.

CHAPTER FIVE

Recommendations

Enhancing Performance Under Stress

The research on stress inoculation and interviews with the Navy and Army suggest that SIT can be an effective strategy for enhancing performance under stress. Although the Air Force currently provides some education (Phase 1 of SIT) to CCTs about the stress response and to PJs about performance enhancement strategies during the Indoctrination Course and sufficient opportunities for CCTs and PJs to practice operational tasks under stressful conditions (Phase 3 of SIT), the Air Force could bolster these efforts with a more programmatic approach to ensuring that all battlefield airmen specialties have the cognitive and behavioral skills (Phase 2 of SIT) that may further enhance performance under stress. These observations lead us to the following nine recommendations for developing a successful program.

Develop Curricula for Stress Inoculation Training with an Emphasis on Core Skills That Facilitate Performance Enhancement

We recommend building on current efforts during the PJ Preparatory/Development and Indoctrination Courses and collaborating with the Departments of the Navy and the Army to develop curricula for developing the behavioral and cognitive skills that can facilitate airmen's performance under stress. These efforts provide excellent examples of training programs that focus on the development of psychological skills, which have been supported by research on performance enhancement. These skills include (1) imagery, (2) attentional focusing, (3) maintaining concentration, (4) controlling anxiety and activation, (5) positive self-talk, and (6) goal-setting (Krane and Williams, 2006).

Particularly important to any change in battlefield airmen training is ensuring that instructors and squadron commanders are committed to the new curriculum. In fact, research suggests that interventions should include plans to educate supervisors or trainers about the effect of stress and the importance of preventative efforts (Nytro et al., 2000). Indeed, senior leadership support is an integral component of organizational change and successful implementation of interventions targeting stress (Nielsen et al., 2010).

Furthermore, the curricula should be developed in coordination with senior instructors from the battlefield airmen community to increase commitment and ensure that lessons are relevant and meaningful to airmen's needs. For example, training provided during initial skills training could focus on coping strategies for decreasing the stress and anxiety associated with particularly challenging training elements. For some airmen, goal-setting may be most appropriate when learning how to segment broad training objectives, whereas others may need to learn strategies to control arousal before participation in water confidence training. For graduates of battlefield airmen training, SIT should attempt to increase the level of specificity with advanced and unit-level training to maximize mission-specific confidence and performance under anticipated and known stressors (e.g., noise, fatigue, security threats, and foreign language communication).

We also recommend that training instructors be provided with SIT. Having developed a working knowledge of SIT, instructors can reinforce these skills during multiple components of training (e.g., parachute, weapons, and dive training).

Identify Opportunities to Integrate Common Stressors from Downrange Experiences

As battlefield airmen return from deployments, attempts should be made to document the specific nature, range, and intensity of stressors. Along these lines, Hall et al. (1992) suggest conducting "a step-by-step stressor analysis, to identify (a) typical stressors encountered, (b) performance deficiencies due to stressors in terms of psychomotor and cognitive processes, (c) knowledge, skills, and abilities (KSAs) required to promote technical performance while exposed to the stressors, and (d) specific cues in the environment that trigger use of effective stress coping skills" (p. 360). Although research has shown that the skills learned during SIT can transfer to novel stressors (Driskell, Johnston, and Salas, 2001), familiarity with the operational environment will help to decrease anxiety, facilitate concentration on task-relevant details, and increase confidence. This recommendation is consistent with Keinan and Friedland's (1996) tenet that "trainees should be given the opportunity to familiarize themselves with stressors characteristic of the criterion situation. Familiarity is needed in order to reduce uncertainty and to improve the transfer of learning" (p. 263). The Air Force currently collects information related to this recommendation (e.g., in the Post Deployment Health Assessment); however, these screening tools are designed primarily to target trauma that may result in severe stress or PTSD. Additional efforts should be made to document other stressors that may affect performance (e.g., noise, sand, and lack of mission clarity).

Ensure That Applicable Skills Are Mastered Before Exposure to Stressful Conditions

Stress inoculation training will be inefficient or ineffective if individuals are unable to successfully perform target job tasks in nonstress conditions. For example, pool harassment to simulate rotor wash will not promote stress inoculation if the individual is not a capable and confident swimmer. On the contrary, exposure to intense stressors before mastery may interfere with the acquisition of skills and may create despair in trainees (Keinan and Friedland, 1996).

We recommend evaluating whether a preparatory course may benefit battlefield airmen candidates. Additionally, we also recommend that evaluations be conducted to determine if the two-week preparatory course for PJ candidates is sufficient for the physical demands of the Indoctrination Course. A longer preparatory course may not only be useful for introducing psychological skills training but may also be used to improve physical conditioning and the development of other necessary physical skills (e.g., swimming). The Navy's significantly longer eight-week preparatory course has been found to significantly decrease the number of drop-on-requests in follow-on BUD/S training.

Provide a Water Training Facility for Pararescue and Combat Control Training

Email correspondence with AETC subject matter experts identified safety issues with the current facility as a result of documented health concerns, including eye, ear, and upper respiratory diseases. These infections also increase the risk of training failure and attrition. Not only are there health concerns with the current facility, but trainees also have limited opportunities to practice water skills in the current facility. With the construction of a new facility, infections attributed to poor water quality would be reduced. Furthermore, trainees could be encouraged to use it during off-duty hours to improve their confidence and technical skills in the water, which would be an important step in implementing an effective SIT program for CCTs and PJs.

Continue to Provide Sufficient Opportunities to Practice New Coping Skills Under "Real" Performance Conditions

Providing opportunities to perform under stress is critical, because in the absence of "the 'inoculation' trials and application opportunities, the skills-training components are unlikely to prove effective or sufficient" (Meichenbaum, 2007, p. 26). Focus groups and interviews with Air Force subject matter experts indicated that ample opportunities were provided in most cases. However, additional opportunities to practice in joint exercises with the Army and Navy may increase awareness of other specific stressors. For example, understanding that different terminology, procedures, and equipment may be encountered in a joint operation may help battlefield airmen to better prepare for these stressors.

Consider Supporting Stress Inoculation Training with Virtual Reality Technology

Several VR models are currently being used to support military training, including the Army Full Spectrum Warrior Game. The Air Force should evaluate the potential modification of these platforms to support training for battlefield airmen. The Air Force could also consider collaborating with ongoing VR-enhanced training experiments such as the Army's VR medical center experiment using aeromedical personnel at Ft. Rucker.

Continue Efforts to Identify Valid Screening Tools to Predict Success in Stressful Conditions

Despite the best efforts to train all airmen to specific standards, considerable individual differences exist in performance under stress (Delahaij et al., 2011). Consequently, selection into a career field for initial skills training is part of a broader strategy for optimizing resources and maximizing opportunities for success. Research evidence reviewed by Szalma (2008) suggests that an individual's traits may affect his performance under stress. However, the specific traits predictive of performance under stress will, at least partially, depend on the tasks being performed.

The Navy has implemented a tool to assess tolerance to stress, which is combined into a compensatory model with physical fitness scores for selection into BUD/S training. In addition to the EQ-I and TAPAS, the Air Force should consider other well-established personnel selection methods such as structured interviews and biodata instruments for predicting success (Hunter and Hunter, 1984; McDaniel et al., 1994; Mount, Witt, and Barrick, 2000; Rothstein et al., 1990; Schmidt and Hunter, 1998; Wright, Lichtenfels, and Pursell, 1989). Interviews conducted by an Air Force psychologist are already being used to select cross-trainees into battlefield airmen careers; however, this practice is not used with new enlistees.

The goal of such screening instruments should be to eliminate only those candidates who cannot train and develop the necessary skills to perform well under stress. Consequently, efforts should be made to set the cutoff for screening instruments at a point that minimizes the elimination of individuals who have the potential to succeed with the right training. This strategy is particularly important to ensure that a sufficient number of operators successfully complete training.

Develop Measures to Support the Evaluation of Screening Tools and SIT

Currently accessible measures, such as attrition and training performance, are useful and informative but may be deficient in determining the effectiveness of SIT. The Air Force should consider expanding measures of training performance to include peer and instructor ratings of other relevant training dimensions (e.g., stress tolerance, performance under stress, and decisionmaking under stress). The Army has made extensive use of peer ratings to support the screening and development of Special Forces. In addition to measuring performance under stress, steps should be taken to evaluate changes in physiological and psychological indicators of arousal when performing under stress. An excellent example using this approach is the Federal Law Enforcement Training Center's (FLETC) study (Atkins and Norris, 2004), which examined law enforcement trainees' performance in a realistic simulation designed to induce stress.[1] Among the criteria measured, FLETC documented physiological values (i.e., heart rate, blood pressure, and salivary cortisol), psychological responses using self-report instruments of personality (e.g., anxiety, anger, depression, and curiosity), and performance evaluated by subject matter experts on several dimensions (e.g., perception, threat recognition, latency to respond, and performance skill scores such as shot accuracy). Similar measures have been used in other realistic scenario-based training (Taverniers et al., 2011).

Additional measures expected to be affected by SIT would also include perceptions of combat readiness. These measures typically assess combat readiness using collective efficacy, or airmen's beliefs about how successful the team will be in future combat. In fact, researchers recommend using combat readiness as a proxy measure for performance, because it has been significantly correlated with objective measures of performance (Thomas, Adler, and Castro, 2005).

In addition to ensuring that relevant measures have been implemented, steps need to be taken to evaluate the effectiveness of SIT. The Air Force might consider implementing a pilot study to examine the relative effectiveness of SIT for improving training outcomes and operational performance. Such a pilot study could use an experimental design with matched groups (i.e., intervention and control groups) based on performance deficits under different stressors. Matching on performance deficits would be particularly important, since stress interventions have been shown to be more effective for those experiencing higher levels of distress at baseline (Flaxman and Bond, 2010).

Provide Information to Increase Awareness of Support Services for Mental Health

Although psychological health and well-being are topics beyond the scope of this study, we would be remiss not to make this recommendation, since these issues were raised without prompting during the focus groups. Similar to concerns raised during interviews with Army subject matter experts, considerable gaps in knowledge were identified in what airmen should do when stress becomes unmanageable. This concern appears not to be limited to the United States, as surveys of international military leaders suggest that international military lead-

---

[1]   To induce stress, FLETC added a variety of structured challenges, including but not limited to environmental distractions such as noise, time pressure, and physical threat with nonlethal training ammunition; multitask loading; and reduced resources such as minimal cover in a firefight and having to use a weapon that had been rigged to misfire.

ers are not sufficiently trained on how to manage individual and family stress (Adler et al., 2008). Consequently, efforts should be bolstered to raise awareness of available support services, including mental health services, chaplains, peer networks, and information websites (e.g., Defense Centers of Excellence for Psychological Health and Traumatic Brain Injury).

Conclusion

Stress is a common element in military careers, especially for those who operate outside the wire. Conventional wisdom suggests that individuals who are selected and succeed in these careers have an inherent ability to withstand stress. Indeed, cognitive ability and certain personality traits have been found, in some contexts, to facilitate performance under stress. However, we also find sufficient evidence that individuals can be trained to minimize the adverse effects of stress on performance. The incorporation of these training techniques, used by the Army and Navy to promote the development of their special operators, would be expected to positively affect the mission readiness of battlefield airmen in several ways, including enhanced performance under stress, reduced attrition during initial skills training, and increased retention.

Interview Guide for Battlefield Airmen

The purpose of this project is to identify whether training strategies to meet stress demands can aid in the training and performance of Battlefield Airmen. So, we will be asking a number of questions related to the types of stressors you face, how you perform under stress, and the types of strategies that you use or have learned to handle stress before, during, and after an operation. As you think about your answers, please remember to **not report any names or classified information**.

Background

- Please describe your level of experience in the Air Force.
- What is your current rank?
- When did you receive your training to be a PJ, CCT, etc.?
- Compared to the number of mission deployments of others in your career field, would you consider yourself less experienced, about the same, or more experienced?

Training Preparation

- What was the most difficult part of your training to become a PJ, CCT, etc.?
  - What strategies did you use to meet the physical and cognitive demands of training?
  - What have you learned since becoming a PJ, CCT, etc. that would have helped you to better meet the physical and cognitive demands of training?
- How are the stressors you faced in training similar to the stressors you face during a mission? How are the stressors in training and during missions different?
- Did any part of your training prepare you for operating in a stressful environment?
  - Please describe.
  - How effective were these training elements?
  - How could these training elements be changed to improve how well individuals perform in a stressful environment?

Stressors

- Please think about your first operation following training.
  - What was most challenging? In what ways could you have been better prepared?
- What are the most stressful components you face in an operational environment?
  - Without providing any names or classified details, please describe a time when the performance (e.g., attention, motivation, motor skills, decision making, communication)

of someone on your team was affected by difficult operational conditions (e.g., weather, heat, time pressure, presence of enemy combatants, etc.).
  ◦ Why do you think this individual's performance was affected?
  ◦ Do you think additional training could have helped? If so, how?
  – Please describe a time when you had to deal with (x stressor).
    ◦ How did you handle this stressor? Did you use any particular strategies?

Future Preparation and Execution

- How confident are you now in being able to perform under a range of stressful conditions?
  – What factors have affected your confidence, either positively or negatively?
- Would you or others in your unit benefit from additional training while experiencing a range of stressful conditions?
  – If so, please describe the types of stressors and tasks (e.g., extraction) that might better prepare you or enhance your performance under stress.

Summary Evaluation

- Overall, how well did your training prepare you to handle the challenges of performing your tasks in a stressful environment?

Interview Guide for Subject Matter Experts

- How is training currently designed to help CCTs/PJs to better perform under stressful conditions?
  - How has the training of CCTs/PJs changed over time?
- What are the most stressful parts of the current training program?
  - At what point in the training cycle do the most stressful parts occur?
  - What do trainees do to meet the demands of these stressors?
    - How well do they meet the demands of these stressors?
  - Are there any specific training modules designed to help trainees meet stressful demands? (e.g., cognitive skills training)
- In what specific ways is stress induced to better prepare CCTs/PJs?
  - Type of stress?
  - Frequency, duration, and intensity of stress?
- Has there been any evaluation on the effectiveness of inducing stress in training CCTs/PJs?
- What types of stressors do CCTs/PJs face in the operational environment?
- How do you think training of CCTs/PJs could incorporate additional exposure to stressful conditions?
  - At what time in the training cycle?
- What factors would affect the implementation of additional training to stressful conditions?

References

Adair, B. (2005). Did the Army get out-gamed? *St. Petersburg Times,* February 20. As of September 30, 2011: http://www.sptimes.com/2005/02/20/Worldandnation/Did_the_Army_get_out_.shtml

Adler, A. B., D. McGurk, M. C. Stetz, and P. D. Bliese (2004). Military Occupational Stressors in Garrison, Training, and Deployed Environments: DTIC Online.

Adler, A. B., P. Cawkill, C. van den Berg, P. Arvers, J. Puente, and Y. Cuvelier (2008). International military leaders' survey on operational stress. *Military Medicine, 173*(1), 10–16.

Air Force Instruction 36-2201 (2002). *Training Development, Delivery, and Evaluation,* Vol. 1, October 1.

Akerstedt, T. (1987). Sleep/wake disturbances in working life. *Electroencephalography and Clinical Neurophysiology. Supplement, 39,* 360.

Atkins, V. J., and W. A. Norris (2004). Survival Scores Research Project: FLETC Research Paper. Glynco, Ga.: Federal Law Enforcement Training Center.

Bar-On, R., J. M. Brown, B. D. Kirkcaldy, and E. P. Thome (2000). Emotional expression and implications for occupational stress: An application of the Emotional Quotient Inventory (EQ-i). *Personality and Individual Differences, 28*(6), 1107–1118.

Barwood, M. J., J. Dalzell, A. K. Datta, R. C. Thelwell, and M. J. Tipton (2006). Breath-hold performance during cold water immersion: Effects of psychological skills training. *Aviation Space and Environmental Medicine, 77*(11), 1136–1142.

Baumann, A., and R. Deber (1989). The limits of decision analysis for rapid decision making in ICU nursing. *Journal of Nursing Scholarship, 21*(2), 69–71.

Bjerner, B. (1949). Alpha depression and lowered pulse rate during delayed actions in a serial reaction test: A study in sleep deprivation. *Acta Physiologica Scandinavica, 19*(Supplement 65), 1–93.

Bonanno, G. A., M. Westphal, and A. D. Mancini (2011). Resilience to loss and potential trauma. *Annual Review of Clinical Psychology, 7,* 511–535.

Burke, S., H. A. Priest, E. Salas, D. Sims, and K. Mayer (2008). Stress and teams: How stress affects decision making at the team level. In J. A. Cannon-Bowers and E. Salas (eds.), *Making Decisions Under Stress: Implications for Individual and Team Training. American Psychological Association,* 181–208.

Cigrang, J. A., S. L. Todd, and E. G. Carbone (2000). Stress management training for military trainees returned to duty after a mental health evaluation: Effect on graduation rates. *Journal of Occupational Health Psychology, 5*(1), 48–55.

Crust, L. (2007). Mental toughness in sport: A review. *International Journal of Sport and Exercise Psychology.*

Curran, M. L., and P. C. Terry (2010). *What you see is what you get: A meta-analytic review of the effects of imagery in sport and exercise domains.* Paper presented at the 27th International Congress of Applied Psychology, Melbourne, Australia.

Delahaij, R., K. van Dam, A.W.K. Gaillard, and J. Soeters (2011). Predicting performance under acute stress: The role of individual characteristics. *International Journal of Stress Management, 18*(1), 49.

Department of the Army (2011). MADN-CSF Memorandum for Record, Subject: Comprehensive Soldier Fitness Performance and Resilience Enhancement Program (CSF-PREP) Executive Summary, May 19.

Dienstbier, R. A. (1989). Arousal and physiological toughness—Implications for mental and physical health. *Psychological Review, 96*(1), 84–100.

Drach-Zahavy, A., and A. Freund (2007). Team effectiveness under stress: A structural contingency approach. *Journal of Organizational Behavior, 28*(4), 423–450. doi: 10.1002/Job.430

Driediger, M., C. Hall, and N. Callow (2006). Imagery use by injured athletes: A qualitative analysis. *Journal of Sports Sciences, 24*(3), 261–271. doi: 10.1080/02640410500128221

Driskell, J. E., C. Copper, and A. Moran (1994). Does mental practice enhance performance? *Journal of Applied Psychology, 79*(4), 481.

Driskell, J. E., and J. H. Johnston (1998). Stress exposure training. In J. A. Cannon-Bowers and E. Salas (eds.), *Making Decisions Under Stress: Implications for Individual and Team Training* (pp. 191–217): American Psychological Association.

Driskell, J. E., J. H. Johnston, and E. Salas (2001). Does stress training generalize to novel settings? *Human Factors: The Journal of the Human Factors and Ergonomics Society, 43*(1), 99–110. doi: 10.1518/001872001775992471

Driskell, J. E., E. Salas, and J. Johnston (1999). Does stress lead to a loss of team perspective? *Group Dynamics: Theory, Research, and Practice, 3*(4), 291.

Driskell, J. E., R. P. Willis, and C. Copper (1992). Effect of overlearning on retention. *Journal of Applied Psychology, 77*(5), 615.

Ellis, A.P.J. (2006). System breakdown: The role of mental models and transactive memory in the relationship between acute stress and team performance. *Academy of Management Journal, 49*(3), 576–589.

Ellis, A., and W. Dryden (1987). *The Practice of Rational-Emotive Therapy (RET)*. New York: Springer Publishing Company.

Ellis, A.P.J., B. S. Bell, R. E. Ployhart, J. R. Hollenbeck, and D. R. Ilgen (2005). An evaluation of generic teamwork skills training with action teams: Effects on cognitive and skill-based outcomes. *Personnel Psychology, 58*(3), 641-672.

Eysenck, M. W., N. Derakshan, R. Santos, and M. G. Calvo (2007). Anxiety and cognitive performance: Attentional control theory. *Emotion, 7*(2), 336–353. doi: 10.1037/1528-3542.7.2.336

Flaxman, P. E., and F. W. Bond (2010). Worksite stress management training: Moderated effects and clinical significance. *Journal of Occupational Health Psychology, 15*(4), 347–358. doi: 10.1037/A0020522

Goel, N., H. Rao, J. S. Durmer, and D. F. Dinges (2009). Neurocognitive consequences of sleep deprivation. *Seminars in Neurology, 29*(4), 320–339. doi: 10.1055/s-0029-1237117

Hall, J. K., J. E. Driskell, E. Salas, and J. A. Cannon-Bowers (1992). *Development of instructional design guidelines for stress exposure training*. Paper presented at the Interservice/Industry Training, Simulation & Education Conference (I/ITSEC).

Hancock, P. A., and J. L. Szalma (eds.) (2008). *Performance Under Stress*. Bodmin, Cornwall: MPG Books Ltd.

Harrison, Y., and J. A. Horne (2000). Sleep loss and temporal memory. *The Quarterly Journal of Experimental Psychology. A, Human Experimental Psychology, 53*(1), 271–279. doi: 10.1080/713755870

Hinshaw, K. E. (1991). The effects of mental practice on motor skill performance: Critical evaluation and meta-analysis. *Imagination, Cognition and Personality*.

Hockey, G.R.J. (1997). Compensatory control in the regulation of human performance under stress and high workload: A cognitive-energetical framework. *Biological Psychology, 45*(1–3), 73–93.

Hunter, J. E., and R. F. Hunter (1984). Validity and utility of alternative predictors of job performance. *Psychological Bulletin, 96*(1), 72.

Johnston, J. H., and J. A. Cannon-Bowers (1996). Training for stress exposure. In J. E. Driskell and E. Salas (eds.), *Stress and Human Performance* (pp. 223–256). Mahwah, N.J.: Erlbaum.

Johnston, J. H., J. E. Driskell, and E. Salas (1997). Vigilant and hypervigilant decision making. *Journal of Applied Psychology, 82*(4), 614.

Jones, L., and G. Stuth (1997). The uses of mental imagery in athletics: An overview. *Applied & Preventive Psychology, 6*(2), 101–115.

Keinan, G., and N. Friedland (1996). Training effective performance under stress: Queries, dilemmas, and possible solutions. In J. E. Driskell and E. Salas (eds.), *Stress and Human Performance* (pp. 257–277). Mahwah, N.J.: Erlbaum.

Kivimaki, M., and S. Lusa (1994). Stress and cognitive performance of fire fighters during smoke diving. *Stress Medicine, 10*(1), 63–68.

Krane, V., and J. M. Williams (2006). Psychological characteristics of peak performance. In J. M. Williams (ed.), *Applied Sport Psychology: Personal Growth to Peak Performance* (pp. 207–227). New York: McGraw-Hill.

Lamontagne, A. D., T. Keegel, A. M. Louie, A. Ostry, and P. A. Landsbergis (2007). A systematic review of the job-stress intervention evaluation literature, 1990–2005. *International Journal of Occupational and Environmental Health, 13*(3), 268–280.

Lazarus, R. S., and S. Folkman (1984). *Stress, Appraisal, and Coping.* New York: Springer Publishing Company.

LePine, J. A., R. F. Piccolo, C. L. Jackson, J. E. Mathieu, and J. R. Saul (2008). A meta-analysis of teamwork processes: Tests of a multidimensional model and relationships with team effectiveness criteria. *Personnel Psychology, 61*(2), 273–307.

Locke, E. A. (1996). Motivation through conscious goal setting. *Applied and Preventive Psychology, 5*(2), 117–124.

Locke, E. A., and G. P. Latham (2002). Building a practically useful theory of goal setting and task motivation. *American Psychologist, 57*(9), 705–717.

Lyons, D. M., K. J. Parker, M. Katz, and A. F. Schatzberg (2009). Developmental cascades linking stress inoculation, arousal regulation, and resilience. *Frontiers in Behavioral Neuroscience, 3.* doi 10.3389/Neuro.08.032.2009

Manacapilli, T., C. M. Hardison, B. Gifford, A. Bailey, and A. Bower (2007). *Common Battlefield Training for Airmen.* Santa Monica, Calif.: RAND Corporation, MG-624-AF. As of November 15, 2012: http://www.rand.org/pubs/monographs/MG624.html

Mathieu, J., M. G. Maynard, T. Rapp, and L. Gilson (2008). Team effectiveness 1997–2007: A review of recent advancements and a glimpse into the future. *Journal of Management, 34*(3), 410–476. doi: 10.1177/0149206308316061

McClernon, C. K. (2009). Stress effects on transfer from virtual environment flight training to stressful flight environments (Tech. Rep. No. ADA-501682). Monterey, Calif.: Naval Postgraduate School.

McClernon, C. K., M. E. McCauley, P. E. O'Connor, and J. S. Warm (2011). Stress training improves performance during a stressful flight. *Human Factors, 53*(3), 207–218. doi: 10.1177/0018720811405317

McDaniel, M. A., D. L. Whetzel, F. L. Schmidt, and S. D. Maurer (1994). The validity of employment interviews: A comprehensive review and meta-analysis. *Journal of Applied Psychology, 79*(4), 599.

McGurk, D., M. C. Stetz, and P. D. Bliese.

Meichenbaum, D. (1985). *Stress Inoculation Training.* New York: Pergamon Press.

Meichenbaum, D. (2007). Stress inoculation training: A preventative and treatment approach. In R. L. Woolfolk and W. S. Sime (eds.), *Principles and Practice of Stress Management* (3rd ed.), pp. 497-518, New York: Guilford Press.

Meredith, L. S., C. D. Sherbourne, S. Gaillot, L. Hansell, H. V. Ritschard, A. M. Parker, and G. Wrenn (2011). *Promoting Psychological Resilience in the U.S. Military,* Santa Monica, Calif.: RAND Corporation, MG-996-OSD. As of November 15, 2012: http://www.rand.org/pubs/monographs/MG996.html

Morris, G. O., H. L. Williams, and A. Lubin (1960). Misperception and disorientation during sleep deprivation. *Archives of General Psychiatry.*

Mount, M. K., L. Witt, and M. R. Barrick (2000). Incremental validity of empirically keyed biodata scales over GMA and the five factor personality constructs. *Personnel Psychology, 53*(2), 299–323.

Nielsen, K., R. Randall, A. L. Holten, and E. R. Gonzalez (2010). Conducting organizational-level occupational health interventions: What works? *Work and Stress, 24*(3), 234–259. doi 10.1080/02678373.2010.519176

Nytro, K., P. O. Saksvik, A. Mikkelsen, P. Bohle, and M. Quinlan, M. (2000). An appraisal of key factors in the implementation of occupational stress interventions. *Work and Stress, 14*(3), 213–225.

Orasanu, J. M., and P. Backer (1996). Stress and military performance. In J. E. Driskell and E. Salas (eds.), *Stress and Human Performance* (pp. 89–126). Mahwah, N.J.: Lawrence Erlbaum Associates.

Pflanz, S., and S. Sonnek (2002). Work stress in the military: Prevalence, causes, and relationship to emotional health. *Military Medicine, 167*(11), 877.

Popovic, S., M. Horvat, D. Kukolja, B. Dropuljic, and K. Cosic (2009). Stress inoculation training supported by physiology-driven adaptive virtual reality stimulation. *Studies in Health Technology and Informatics, 144,* 50–54.

Riva, G. (2005). Virtual reality in psychotherapy: Review. *CyberPsychology & Behavior, 8*(3), 220–240.

Riva, G. (2006). Being-in-the-word-with: Presence meets social and cognitive neuroscience. In G. Riva, M. T. Anguera, B. K. Wiederhold, and F. Mantovani (eds.), *From Communication to Presence: Cognition, Emotions and Culture Towards the Ultimate Communicative Experience* (pp. 47–80). Amsterdam: IOS Press.

Riva, G. (2007). Virtual reality and telepresence. *Science, 318*(5854), 1240.

Riva, G. (2008). From virtual to real body: Virtual reality as embodied technology. *Journal of CyberTherapy & Rehabilitation, 1*(1), 7.

Riva, G., F. Davide, and W. A. IJsselsteijn (2003). *Being there: Concepts, Effects and Measurements of User Presence in Synthetic Environments* (Vol. 5): Amsterdam: IOS Press.

Riva, G., J. A. Waterworth, and E. Waterworth (2004). The layers of presence: A bio-cultural approach to understanding presence in natural and mediated environments. *Cyberpsychology & Behavior, 7*(4), 402–416.

Rizzo, A., J. Pair, K. Graap, B. Manson, P. J. McNerney, B. Wiederhold, and J. Spira (2006). A virtual reality exposure therapy application for Iraq War military personnel with post traumatic stress disorder: From training to toy to treatment. *NATO Security Through Science Series E Human and Societal Dynamics 6,* 235.

Rohrer, D., K. Taylor, H. Pashler, J. T. Wixted, and N. J. Cepeda (2005). The effect of overlearning on long term retention. *Applied Cognitive Psychology, 19*(3), 361–374.

Rothstein, H. R., F. L. Schmidt, F. W. Erwin, W. A. Owens, and C. P. Sparks (1990). Biographical data in employment selection: Can validities be made generalizable? *Journal of Applied Psychology, 75*(2), 175.

Saunders, T., J. E. Driskell, J. H. Johnston, and E. Salas (1996). The effect of stress inoculation training on anxiety and performance. *Journal of Occupational Health Psychology, 1*(2), 170–186.

Schmidt, F. L., and J. E. Hunter (1998). The validity and utility of selection methods in personnel psychology: Practical and theoretical implications of 85 years of research findings. *Psychological Bulletin, 124*(2), 262.

Seery, M. D., E. A. Holman, and R. C. Silver (2010). Whatever does not kill us: Cumulative lifetime adversity, vulnerability, and resilience. *Journal of Personality and Social Psychology, 99*(6), 1025–1041. doi: 10.1037/a0021344

Sheehy, R., and J. J. Horan (2004). Effects of stress inoculation training for 1st-year law students. *International Journal of Stress Management, 11*(1), 41.

Smith, D., C. Wright, A. Allsopp, and H. Westhead (2007). It's all in the mind: PETTLEP-based imagery and sports performance. *Journal of Applied Sport Psychology, 19*(1), 80–92.

Staal, M. A. (2004). Stress, cognition, and human performance: A literature review and conceptual framework. *NASA Technical Memorandum,* 212824. Moffett Field, Calif.: Ames Research Center.

Stetz, M. C., C. P. Long, W. V. Schober, Jr., C. G. Cardillo, and R. M. Wildzunas (2007a). Stress assessment and management while medics take care of the VR wounded. *Annual Review of CyberTherapy and Telemedicine, 5*, 165–171.

Stetz, M. C., M. L. Thomas, M. B. Russo, T. A. Stetz, R. M. Wildzunas, J. J. McDonald, and J. A. Romano (2007b). Stress, mental health, and cognition: A brief review of relationships and countermeasures. *Aviation, Space, and Environmental Medicine, 78*(Supplement 1), B252–B260.

Steuer, J. (1992). Defining virtual reality: Dimensions determining telepresence. *Journal of Communication, 42*(4), 73–93.

Szalma, J. L. (2008). Individual differences in stress reactions. In P. A. Hancock and J. L. Szalma (eds.), *Performance Under Stress* (pp. 323–358). Bodmin, Cornwall: MPG Books Ltd.

Tanielian, T. L., L. Jaycox, D. M. Adamson, M. A. Burnam, R. M. Burns, L. B. Caldarone, R. A. Cox, E. J. D'Amico, C. Diaz, C. Eibner, G. Fisher, T. C. Helmus, B. R. Karney, B. Kilmer, G. N. Marshall, L. T. Martin, L. S. Meredith, K. N. Metscher, K. C. Osilla, R. L. Pacula, R. N. Ramchand, J. S. Ringel, T. L. Schell, J. M. Sollinger, M. E. Vaiana, K. M. Williams, and M. R. Yochelson (2008). *Invisible Wounds of War: Psychological and Cognitive Injuries, Their Consequences, and Services to Assist Recovery*, Santa Monica, Calif.: RAND Corporation, MG-720-CCF. As of November 15, 2012: http://www.rand.org/pubs/monographs/MG720.html

Taverniers, J., T. Smeets, J. Van Ruysseveldt, J. Syroit, and J. von Grumbkow, J. (2011). The risk of being shot at: Stress, cortisol secretion, and their impact on memory and perceived learning during reality-based practice for armed officers. *International Journal of Stress Management, 18*(2), 113.

Thomas, J. L., A. B. Adler, and C. A. Castro (2005). Measuring operations tempo and relating it to military performance. *Military Psychology, 17*(3), 137–156.

Torsvall, L., and T. Akerstedt (1987). Sleepiness on the job: Continuously measured EEG changes in train drivers. *Electroencephalography and Clinical Neurophysiology, 66*(6), 502–511.

U.S. Air Force (2010). Combat Control fact sheet. August 18. As of September 26, 2011: http://www.af.mil/information/factsheets/factsheet.asp?id=174

U.S. Air Force (2012). Pararescue fact sheet. February 1. As of September 26, 2011: http://www.af.mil/information/factsheets/factsheet.asp?id=1

Walker, M. P. (2010). Sleep, memory and emotion. *Progress in Brain Research, 185*, 49–68. doi: 10.1016/B978-0-444-53702-7.00004-X

West, D. J., J. J. Horan, and P. A. Games (1984). Component analysis of occupational stress inoculation applied to registered nurses in an acute care hospital setting. *Journal of Counseling Psychology, 31*(2), 209–218.

Wiederhold, B., and M. Wiederhold (2008). Virtual reality for posttraumatic stress disorder and stress inoculation training. *Journal of CyberTherapy & Rehabilitation, 1*(1), 37–48.

Wiederhold, M., and B. Wiederhold (2005). *Military mental health applications*. Paper presented at the 13th Annual Medicine Meets Virtual Reality Conference, Long Beach, Calif.

Williams, H. L., A. Lubin, and J. J. Goodnow (1959). Impaired performance with acute sleep loss. *Psychological Monographs*.

Wright, P. M., P. A. Lichtenfels, and E. D. Pursell (1989). The structured interview: Additional studies and a meta-analysis. *Journal of Occupational Psychology, 62*(3), 191–199.

Young, J. A. (2008). *The Effects of Life-Stress on Pilot Performance*. Moffet Field, Calif.: Ames Research Center.